*Education and
Democratic Theory*

SUNY series, Democracy and Education
George H. Wood, editor
and
SUNY series in Political Theory: Contemporary Issues
Philip Green, editor

Education and Democratic Theory:

Finding A Place for Community Participation in Public School Reform

A. Belden Fields
and
Walter Feinberg

with the assistance of Nicole Roberts

State University of New York Press

Published by
State University of New York Press, Albany

For information, address State University of New York Press,
90 State Street, Suite 700, Albany, NY 12207

Production by Judith Block
Marketing by Fran Keneston

Library of Congress Cataloging-in-Publication Data

Fields, A. Belden.
    Education and democratic theory : finding a place for community participa-
tion in public school reform / A. Belden Fields and Walter Feinberg with the
assistance of Nicole Roberts.
    p. cm. — (SUNY series, democracy and education) (SUNY series in political
theory. Contemporary issues)
Includes bibliographical references and index.
ISBN 0–7914–4999–8 (alk. paper) — ISBN 0–7914–5000–7 (pbk. : alk. paper)
1. Public schools—United States—Citizen participation—Case studies.
2. Community and school—United States—Case studies. 3. Educational
change—United States—Citizen participation—Case studies. I. Feinberg,
Walter, 1937– . II. Roberts, Nicole. III. Title. IV. Series. V. Series:
SUNY series in political theory. Contemporary issues.

LC221.F54 2001
370'.973—dc21   00–061925

10 9 8 7 6 5 4 3 2 1

To those who have been struggling for
a more inclusive and equitable system
of public education in Ed City

Contents

Acknowledgments

We wish to acknowledge the support of the Research Board of the University of Illinois at Urbana/Champaign. The diligent work of Nicole Roberts, our research assistant, was invaluable. Our appreciation to Norman Denzin for his work on the initial phase of this project and for the help he provided in informing the methodological aspects of our research. Our thanks as well to Jason Odeshoo for his assistance as we edited the manuscript and to Phyllis Koerner for the superior job of formatting the final version of the manuscript before we sent it off to SUNY Press. We also want to thank the people in Ed City who both welcomed us into their city and encouraged our work.

Introduction

The Focus of the Study

As the title indicates, this book is about both education, and more precisely public education, and democratic theory. It is a theoretical work, about the relationships between education and democracy in a multicultural setting in which educational inequality exists between racial groups. In this study we draw upon interviews and observations which we conducted over a span of about four years. In this book we want to demonstrate the importance of the relationship between concrete experience and theoretical understandings. The concrete experience is that of educational activists in a community that we call Ed City.* The theoretical concern is the extent to which differing conceptions of democracy enable participation from members of diverse racial groups.

In this study the idea of Site-Based Decision Making (SBDM) dominates the early discourse of many of the key actors in Ed City, but the reader should be cautioned that this is not a study of SBDM. Rather, it is an analysis of the conceptions of democracy and education that the use of the term implies and of evolution that takes place as other notions of democracy are introduced into the mix.

The reader should also be cautioned that this is not an implementation study. Quite the contrary, we stop our study just at the point that implementation is about to begin. Our interest is rather in understanding the process by which a group of people decides that the public school system must be rendered more democratic and more inclusive,

---

*Ed City is obviously a pseudonym, as are the names we have given to the participants and the Ed City newspapers.

1

how they move from an initial commitment to that aim to action directed to bring it about, and how a variety of community groups and individuals, the school board, and the school administration react to this effort.

Representation and Participation

In addition to the concepts of education and democracy, three other concepts are critical in this study. They are representation, participation, and authority. In any large-scale system of decision making representation is essential. In our political system it is manifested not just in the election of people at the national level where direct participation would be almost impossible, but at the local levels as well where the modern division of labor has removed many people from direct participation in the affairs of government. Those who are critical of the policies that emanate from representative systems can fault them for three reasons. First, following Rousseau, they can question whether representation itself is capable of rendering the community the best policies. Second, they can question whether the specific form of representation practiced in that time and place is the best for the community as a whole or for certain subgroups within it. Third, they can argue that it fails to provide the day to day, issue to issue interaction that binds a community together and enables the different segments to understand their different needs and life experiences. This problem is exacerbated, when, as in Ed City, a group continues to be underrepresented in the decision-making process.

The obverse of representation is direct participation, that is, representing oneself is to be done through civic organizations and movements. A group or movement can attempt to give everyone who cares to participate relatively equal weight in determining goals, strategies, and tactics. This kind of direct participation is usually designed to force a change in policies or systems of decision making. In our study of such a group, the Project for Educational Democracy (PED), the group attempts to mobilize people into active participatory roles outside of the formal system and to change the formal system of educational decision making so that it is more inclusive of people who have not had a say in the education of their children.

Given what some see as a widening gap between the public and what are supposed to be its schools, participation is sometimes seen as the crucial missing link. This is not only a professional reflection which has been largely responsible for the SBDM movement since the mid-

1980s; it also appears to be a view widely held by the public. In a 1999 national survey designed to assess support for public schools, the Horace Mann Educators Corporation found that "ninety-four percent of those surveyed said that all adults in a community—not just parents — should volunteer time, resources or expertise to schools." Although this study found that increased parental participation in the school was judged to be the single most important factor that could make schools more effective, fewer than one-third of those with children in school said that they spent time helping teachers and only 25 percent were active in PTAs.[1] In addition, in both a functioning church-run African American school in Ed City, and in a newer proposal to create a second private African American school in the area, parent participation is stipulated as a requirement if one wishes to enroll and keep one's children in the school. However, participation in these cases is largely confined to helping teachers and administrators in carrying out classroom or school activities. The PED, however, is a movement looking for participation in a deeper sense than helping teachers and participating in an auxiliary organization such as the PTA. It wants to see community members, parent and nonparent, actually participating in the making of decisions and in the assumption of responsibility for them. This brings us to our third crucial concept, authority.

Authority

School boards claim authority through the electoral mechanism. When members of the community have elected them, we can say that they have authorized them to make decisions that other people are not entitled to make. Authority can be delegated. The school board hires a superintendent and delegates to him or her the ability to make authoritative administrative decisions and to feed information and policy recommendations to the school board to provide a basis for its own decisions. This is an important exercise of authority. Teachers exercise authority on the basis of professional training and credentials that have been generated within the controlling political and educational systems themselves.

---

1. Horace Mann Companies (Springfield, Ill.) commissioned survey, conducted by Market Facts, Inc., Telenation, 20–22 August 1999. Available from <jfuller@marketfacts.com>.

Those who call for greater participation do so with the intent of opening up opportunity for those who are not included within the presently operating system. But along with opportunity for some, there are usually at least perceived risks for others. When claims are made from those inside the system to change the patterns of authority (e.g., teachers claiming a share of authority held by administrators), there are risks for both the claimants and the possessors of authority under the status quo. When claims are made by those completely outside the system (e.g., religious fundamentalists trying to impose curriculum or book choices), there are risks to the insiders (teachers, administrators, and board members) but the inertia of the system usually prevails. When the claims are made by those both inside and outside the system, the risk level to both established authority (loss of control and authority) and change agents (retaliation and co-optation) rises. The PED was just such an inside-and-outside movement. A very important part of our story is how the opportunities and the risks were dealt with by both the traditional holders of authority and the members of the PED. We believe that the story of the PED and its efforts will be valuable to those in other communities, both outsiders and insiders in the educational systems, who genuinely seek to close gaps between the public and its schools.

The Background of the Project

For us, it all began with a phone call. In the fall of 1994, Belden Fields received a call from Jerry Mann, a former student in the 1960s who had moved to another city. Jerry, who had become the regional director of a teachers' union, called Belden to arrange a meeting.† Over lunch, Jerry mentioned to Belden that after very bitter negotiations and a teachers' strike that summer, the union and the school board had signed an agreement that he hoped would lead to much greater participation in decision making at the school sites.

The agreement, in the form of a "letter of understanding" appended to the contract, authorized the formation of a committee in 1996–1997 to "summarize" within three years "the practice and procedures" of SBDM across the district. It also authorized the committee to "develop [a] philosophy . . . that reflects our mission and strategic plan." The strategic plan referred to was one developed in 1990 under an earlier superintendent who was a strong advocate of SBDM. The letter spec-

---

† For most of this study we use surnames except when the setting is better reproduced by the use of first names.

ified that the committee was to have "full representation of faculty, staff, administration, students, parents, and community."

Jerry told Belden that he was particularly interested in the involvement of people who had been heretofore excluded, saying that he did not want to see just affluent people involved, and he talked about both working-class people and the African American population being brought into the process. In order to ensure that these voices would be included in the future, he said that a new community organizational effort was being launched. This was the PED. He said that the union had hired an African American organizer, Frank Johnson, to make contacts on the PED's behalf with African American groups in the city. Jerry was concerned about a growing skepticism toward public education and declared that "if changes are not made from the bottom-up democratically, then they are going to be imposed from the top-down." He expressed the belief that such changes would be to the detriment of the teachers and to the community generally, especially those whose voices are presently excluded.

From what Jerry had told him, Belden believed that the project had very interesting implications for democratic theory, and asked Jerry if he and Walter Feinberg, an educational philosopher, might study the process as it evolved. There was a subsequent meeting of the three of us where Jerry laid out his own vision in more detail. It involved a school system where the powers of the school board were devolved to largely autonomous site-based units. The inclusive and participatory elements of his vision particularly caught our interest.

Walter agreed to join the project. He suggested that Norman Denzin, an ethnomethodologist, also be asked to join us, which Norman did until added university responsibilities required more of his attention and thus his leaving the project. We received funds from the University of Illinois's Research Board, which enabled us to hire Nicole Roberts, a graduate student in Educational Policy Studies and a former teacher, to serve as the research assistant for three years.

Initially, there was a certain ambiguity and confusion regarding our role. At one very early meeting of the PED we were introduced as "consultants" and we tried to explain that we were researchers rather than consultants. Yet this confession did not come all that easily, partly because we were, after all, present at Jerry's invitation and the good will of the PED, and partly because we could not see at the very beginning all the nuances of this distinction. Some of these would emerge only as the project evolved and the PED, with us tagging along, came into contact with other groups.

Role Ambiguity: Researchers or Consultants

In this early stage, there was a good bit of ambivalence in our own minds concerning the rather fine distinction between "consultant" and "researcher." We did value the PED's commitments to inclusiveness and participation and surely wanted to see those goals furthered in some form. However, we did not believe that it was appropriate for us to take on the PED as a client whose project we, as "consultants," were dedicated to advancing.

There were two reasons for our reluctance. First, just as the PED did not want to impose its values on the community, a concern that we describe in detail in chapter 3, we did not want to project our under-standings or values onto the process in a way that would steer it one way or another. This was not always easy and the calls were often rather diffi-cult. The second reason involves an implicit distinction that we felt but which we were only able to articulate as the project advanced. As we mentioned, our study required us to move outside the circle of the PED and engage with other groups in the community that were also active in the educational arena. As we did so, we began to appreciate the com-plexity of the situation and to see that although many groups felt the need for more democratic schools, not all of them defined "democracy" in the same way.

Thus, we began to understand the source of our initial hesitation. While a "consultant" has a responsibility to advance the project of the client, a "researcher" has a responsibility to advance knowledge and understanding for an audience that goes beyond the immediate situa-tion. In addition, as "researchers" we had a responsibility to listen to dif-ferent stories and not to privilege one over another without providing good and public reasons. We therefore interviewed individuals and rep-resentatives of groups that had other visions and they have become part of our story. Nevertheless, it was the participatory and inclusive vision of the PED with which we were sympathetic that led us to conduct this study.

Although we saw ourselves as researchers more than consultants, there were times when we tried to be helpful and perhaps came close to the role of unpaid consultants. At other times we felt an urge to pull back from intervening in the process lest we begin to steer that which we hoped to study and intrude on the autonomy of the activists. Sometimes there was what seemed to us to be an easy blending of the two roles and we had no difficulty performing as researcher/consultants. However, we also felt a strong moral ambivalence about our role and often debated how much we should share with the group that had invited us to conduct the study and had opened up their meetings to us. The gracious invitation to conduct the study required that we extend our help where we could. However, there was not always agreement, either among ourselves or between ourselves and some members of the PED, as to what this requirement meant and how it could be served. Thus, for example, one person in the group chided us at a certain point in the study, saying, "That's okay, they'll get their articles from it," believing that we had insights that we were not sharing which could help the process move ahead. She clearly felt that we were objectifying her and the other participants, adopting a clear "we-observer" position looking at "them-observed" participants. At that point, we felt ourselves looked at as ingrates pretending to a superior position who were not paying back an obligation. Our work on race, as will be seen in chapters 4 and 5, led us to a better understanding of how sharply nonverbal communication such as a look that is based upon differential positions can sting. This was an uncomfortable moment for us. But we did not feel that we could simply eliminate all differences between ourselves and PED activists and still continue to do the research.

We were not just neutral observers, either. We applauded the efforts to effect greater inclusiveness and more participation, but sometimes the meetings would stray from these goals. When they did it was often by leaving out a constituency, sometimes members of the community, or students. Since we had the advantage of being the only people at the meeting taking notes, we were often the only ones aware of the drift of the conversation. Yet for us to remind the participants of the turn the discussion had taken sometimes would have exerted a pressure that advanced the goal that we most favored. This became somewhat critical when deliberations moved from the informal PED to the more formally constituted district-wide committee that appeared approximately two years into the process that the PED had initiated.

In fact, there was yet a third reason that we were uncomfortable with the "consultant" designation. We simply did not carry the expertise that the label "consultant" would have thrust upon us. Neither of us pretends to be an expert on K-12 educational systems. But we could lend some perspective to their work. We obliged requests for help when: we felt that we had the competence to be of help; we felt that we were not becoming partisans on issues of contention within the PED or between the PED and other organizations or school officials; and, as already stated, when we felt that our assistance would not push the process in one direction or another. We had explored the educational history of Ed City and had some understanding of the larger social forces that affected movements like this. However, this is certainly not the kind of knowledge required to set the direction or steer the process. When we did share information, for example of an historical nature, we did not restrict our sharing of that information to the PED. Because we systematically took notes and made tapes of meetings and paid careful attention to them, we sometimes served the PED as a source of historical information on their own discussions and decisions. But we did the same for the district-wide committee as well. The dialogues, and sometimes even arguments, among us as we tried to navigate this course between "consultants" and "neutral, objective observers" were often as enlightening for us as were the dynamics we were observing. But it is the latter to which this book is devoted. We now turn to an overview of its contents.

Chapter Outline

Chapter One: Democracy in Small Places. We describe the origins of the PED and its relation to the union, develop some of the conditions that led to its creation, and analyze the PED's initial attempt to grapple with the idea of SBDM as a concept of community empowerment.

Chapter Two: A Failed Attempt. We describe Ed City, the school district in which the study takes place, and the failed attempt of an earlier superintendent to initiate a more participatory form of decision making in the schools. In exploring the reasons for this failure the chapter develops some of the inherent tensions involved in viewing public schools as instruments of participatory decision making.

Chapter Three: Engaging in Democratic Discourse Democratically. Using an early community meeting called by the PED, we explore different views about the best way to advance the ideals of participation and inclusion. We analyze one attempt to do so in a way that the PED feels is consistent with the need to avoid imposition.

Chapter Four: Race and School in Ed City. We examine the history of race relations in Ed City, the community in which the PED operates, in order to understand what it means to be an "underrepresented minority" in a solid, liberal-minded community. We raise the question whether democratic forms of governance should be concerned with group interests as opposed to simply individual ones, and we use this history to show some reasons why, to use the words of Cornell West, "race matters."

Chapter Five: The PED's Challenge to Traditional Authority: The School Board. Through the dialogue between the PED, the school board, and other members of the community we highlight and analyze three different concepts: the underrepresented minority; the best interest of children; and The Ed City way. We show how these different ideas guide educational discourse in Ed City; we examine their connection to broader concerns of democratic theory and show the way in which, as unexamined assumptions held by different parties, they can lead to misunderstanding and miscommunication.

Chapter Six: The Meeting of Bureaucratic and Dialogical Authority: The District Committee. We analyze the dynamics when those who are concerned with the "abstraction" called the "public good," meet those who are concerned with the abstraction called the "real people," the ideal modality of which is a democratic, horizontal, and dialogical form of communication (which is what PED gatherings strive to attain). The setting for this convergence of abstractions is a group formally called the District Site-Based Decision Making Committee. It is a body called by the superintendent, containing PED members, teachers, parents, administrators, board members, and sometimes students, to make a recommendation to the school board regarding decision making in the Ed City schools.

Chapter Seven: Cooperation and Co-optation. We analyze the problems of co-optation, accountability, and authority that arise in different ways for both members of the PED and members of the school administration.

Chapter Eight: Conclusion: Competing Conceptions of Democratic Education and Theory. We analyze what turned out to be a significant but initially imperceptible shift from the systems level of change that the PED had initially intended and worked for, to the level of the individual school. We review some of the accomplishments that the PED nevertheless achieved along the way, and highlight some of the very sticky problems associated with attempts to bring members of previously excluded segments of the community into educational decision making, relating these concerns to some fundamental issues of democratic theory.

CHAPTER ONE

Democracy in Small Places

The Project for Educational Democracy (PED) fits nicely Tocqueville's ideal of the voluntary, noninstitutionalized, face to face, perhaps altruistic body that both within itself and with its mission reflects a certain idea about how democracy should operate. It represents the coming together of a group of citizens from different backgrounds, different races, classes, and religious affiliations to deliberate about the prospects for improving the responsiveness of public education to community concerns. In its concern to include the voices of parents and community members, and especially of people of color and the poor, at the very beginning of its deliberations about the process of decision making, the PED differs from a number of other attempts to "democratize" the schools.

The PED is composed of teachers, parents, students, and community members. Its core, which has changed over the years, is small, about twenty members, although the term *member* is problematic. No one pays dues, no elections are held, meetings are open to anyone who chooses to attend, and some people come and stay while others come and go. Thus, it is hard to say just what constitutes membership other than the time and willingness to attend meetings, especially the planning meetings. Given these loose requirements, given that some members belong to the teachers' union, two to the school board, that some represent themselves and others represent this or that group, it is even hard to say just what constitutes the boundaries of the PED. They are open, one might even say fuzzy.

Nevertheless, some things can be said: the majority of those attending these meetings are teachers, a reasonable number are parents—a number that increases considerably at the group's community meetings. The majority are also white and middle class, but perhaps a quarter of its "membership" at any one time is African American and they too increase considerably at the community meetings, often constituting a majority. It has, at different times, involved larger segments of the community, and some of its members share affiliations with the union and the school board. Moreover, representatives from various local organizations often attend the PED's community meetings.

The PED as an organization is open ended and not neatly defined. For the organization this means that players come and go, that institutional memory is ad hoc, that old ground is traveled over frequently because the value of inclusion and participation is paramount. It also means that its vision of educational democracy, which it refers to as Site-Based Decision Making (SBDM), gives high priority to process over product and to inclusion and participation over a clear statement of goals. And yet, surprisingly perhaps, things do move and the PED has been the principal instrument for moving the formal organs along on its path to some form of increased participation. Although the concept still remains vague and contentious, the PED has succeeded in providing a focal point around which a considerable amount of the energy of the school is being organized.

SBDM, although quite a buzz word in education circles, is open ended, the less polite word is *vague*, and has a number of possible meanings. Part of this study involves how this concept is shaped and reformed through formal and informal negotiation with others in the community. Although SBDM is open to a variety of interpretations, it is intended to indicate the devolution of authority and decision making to the "individual schools." Just what "the individual schools" mean in this context is a part of the informal negotiation. To some the principal is the proper stand-in for the school and should be authorized to make all decisions. To others it is the principal and the teachers, and to still others the school belongs to the parents as well.

Throughout its deliberations the PED has tended to hold to a very broad understanding of the "ownership" of the individual school, wanting to involve not just all of the above, but school staff and members of the community as well, in some form of governing body. And, in the middle and high schools, it wants to include students too.

Members of the PED distinguish SBDM from site-based "management" and identify it with greater participation of parents and community as well as teachers and support staff in the governance of individual local schools. They believe that wider participation is an important and neglected feature of democratic public education. They also believe that with more decision making placed at the school level, schools will see a higher degree of participation on the part of minority group members and poor people and as a result they expect that many educational inequities in their community will be addressed. Yet in one area, most everyone agrees: they do not want decisions about the firing of teachers or administrators to be done by participatory committees or councils in the individual schools. Teachers fear that the price they would pay in reduced solidarity is not worth the extra empowerment that such a shift in authority would bring.

Although the PED has received some encouragement from the administration and school board, the messages are mixed, and clearly not everyone shares its conception of how schools should be run in a democratic society. Some members of the school board as well as a number of teachers and community members are reasonably content with the system as it is, believing that a board elected by the community at large is best equipped to establish policy in a system of this size. Many members of the administration and probably a good number of teachers would voice significant concern if they felt that localized community decision making would threaten their professional prerogatives. And some believe that the system already has SBDM, especially when compared to other systems.

The PED views itself as fighting for the public school ideal. The ideal represents to them participation, inclusiveness, and equal opportunity. Given this ideal, schools have a special role in American society— they prepare all to be active citizens, although the PED realizes that real schools too often ignore or violate this role.

Although the PED fits Tocqueville's ideal in that all members are volunteers, nothing is quite that pure any longer and some, especially those not in tune with SBDM, see it as a child of the teachers' union. And indeed, it was formed at the initiation of the union regional director, Jerry Mann. Moreover, the one paid staff member, the community organizer, is an employee of the union. We will discuss this ambiguous relation later as we talk about some of the boundary characteristics of this group. Yet to see it as just a child of the union misses a lot.

The idea of SBDM has been supported nationally by business as well as unions and PED members view themselves as largely autonomous. The PED has held some meetings at union headquarters, but many members do not belong to the union. It took considerable pains to hold its community meetings in public spaces or in spaces associated with local African American groups. Jerry Mann had a major role in establishing the PED and moderated its early meetings but he has since stepped back as other members have taken on leadership roles. He continues to have a strong interest in its work, but has never countered one of its decisions, and it is questionable whether he is really in a position to do so. His hands-off approach was especially significant in establishing the independence of the PED during early stages when questions of strategy arose and the group took off in directions that he questioned.

The Issue of Centralized Control

Whatever the particular form of SBDM, some people fear that it creates too much autonomy for the local school and threatens to disrupt systematized standards and procedures across a district. Some people defend a more centralized mode of decision making (employing the same standardized tests, the same textbooks, the same scheduling, the same standards for hiring personnel, the same ratios of professional to nonprofessional staff and of teachers to students), believing that it provides an additional layer of protection for professional teachers and administrators from outside pressures, and mutes political and educational differences. Where board members are elected at large, it also provides a ready made argument for legitimizing the board on the grounds that each member has in mind "the interests of all the children in the community."

Yet the PED fears that a centralized system isolates marginalized groups and inhibits them from gaining a voice in the schools thus serving to increase alienation and inequality within and between segments of the community. It wants to find a way to include the voice of these groups in the deliberative process, but how to identify these voices and how to include them in the process is a more complex question than it may appear on the surface. This is the question that the PED has obliged the school board and the administration to address. How can educational and political systems respond when noncorrupt representational systems result consistently in the exclusion of major segments of the community from educational decision-making bodies, and why is such a response important?

The second part of this question may be puzzling from two radically different points of view. From the point of view of the included it may seem puzzling just because a noncorrupt representational system means that everyone has a chance to voice their preference for those who would represent them, and that some have won and others lost. While there may not be a consensus about each and every winner and loser, in a democracy there is a consensus around the process itself. This is exactly what representative democracy means.

Yet, from the point of view of those whose will is consistently overridden or who have learned that voting makes little difference to them the question is puzzling for a different reason. Surely, if a "representational system" results continually in nonrepresentation for a sizable group of people, then it is not truly representational, perhaps not even noncorrupt in some deep sense. And when the children of those who are not represented continue to have lower achievement rates and higher drop out suspension, expulsion, and incarceration rates, the costs of nonrepresentation are visible day after day.

The question, as it is asked above, addresses only part of the story that we want to tell. Representation signals different things to different people. To some it signals a way to elect the best people, with the most foresight, and with the widest public interest in mind. It is a way to select people who will make good decisions. And, when decisions are made that are less than good, people can be voted out of office.[1] Others believe that the word should signal structures of inclusiveness and participation. Those who are elected should represent communities of participants, people who look, act, or think in ways that are similar to those elected.[2] Here, representation is only a stand-in for structures of direct participation, and where these structures are lacking, there is a need to build and maintain them.

We will see that each of these implies very different structures for school governance. The first involves finding the most "civic minded," "best educated" people to run for office and guide the system. We call this the "public good" conception of education. Here, participation from below is individualized and episodic. Ideally it involves an altruistic and knowledgeable elite responding on an issue-by-issue basis, and with the good of the community foremost in mind, to individual grievances and issues brought up from below. The second, which we will call the "real people" model of governance involves devolving as many decisions as possible to the grass roots level, to teachers, parents, staff, and community members. In this model, involvement in the process of decision making has a positive effect on the quality of decisions made and is part of the education of the decision makers. As participation grows, it is

---

1. The classical proponent of this view of representation is Edmund Burke. A twentieth century proponent who has been very influential in the discipline of political science is Joseph Schumpeter, especially his *Capitalism, Socialism, and Democracy* (New York: Harper, 1942).

2. See Anne Phillips, *The Politics of Presence* (Oxford: Clarendon Press, 1995); Iris Young, *Justice and the Politics of Difference* (Princeton: Princeton University Press, 1990); and Charles Taylor, "The Politics of Recognition," in Amy Gutmann, ed., *Multiculturalism* (Princeton: Princeton University Press, 1994).

believed, so does the quality of grass roots decision making. This is the path that the PED has chosen to advance. In the chapters that follow we explore and analyze these viewpoints both from a theoretical standpoint and in terms of the path that the evolution of the PED and its ideas take as it comes into contact with the extended political and educational environment of Ed City. As a way to track these interactions, we begin below with our account of the early history of the PED and our involvement with it.

Defining, Controlling, Speaking, and Toning

The story of the PED begins with the union stimulating the move toward SBDM. The bitter strike had resulted in the somewhat ambiguously worded letter of understanding, attached after the signatures to the contract. The letter noted that a committee would be formed to "summarize" site-based practices in the district. The letter did not mention the union and to our unschooled eyes it appeared to be little more than an expression of interest in exploring aspects of site-based decision making.

To Jerry Mann, however, it had all the signs of a commitment to SBDM. As he tried to steer the process in its early phase, he acted as if the decision to advance a new form of governance had already been made and that all that remained was the implementation. Thus, by defining what it meant "to summarize," Mann seemed to assure that the union would play a major role in the direction that SBDM took. He also expressed a clear vision of what that implementation would look like and how to go about achieving it.

Mann wanted a governance structure in which the school board delegated power to site-based councils, which would make decisions for their schools. He wanted the support staff, another group he represented, included in these councils as full participants along with teachers, parents, and community members. He understood this might be difficult given that teachers are sometimes hostile to janitors, aides, and cafeteria workers but he wanted to change that.

There were dangers that the union needed to be concerned about as well. He spoke of the need to avoid "Creeping Yeshivism," referring to the loss of faculty bargaining rights at Yeshiva University on the grounds that the faculty made management decisions. Hence, he wanted to let the administration continue to do the hiring and firing of personnel. At an early meeting of union representatives Mann sketched out a three-year process for implementing SBDM. He exhorted the area representatives, telling them emphatically that "if we can't do it, the district will and that there will be problems if management does it in a top-down way."

Yet the low percentage of teacher participation in the project continued throughout the PED's history and it was never clear whether the majority of teachers in the district shared Mann's enthusiasm. As in many other movements the work was carried forward by a relatively small number of people even as it gained visibility within the community. Hence, while the majority of teachers did not express any active resistance to the idea of shared decision making, it is unclear whether many supported it enthusiastically. In light of silence on an issue, it is not unusual for leaders to define what the membership wants. Indeed, this is perhaps the major role of leadership, but as we shall see in subsequent chapters, the ethics of speaking for others becomes a major issue for those actively involved in the PED.

Groups must constantly negotiate the issue of tone, depending on whom they wish to include and whom, if anyone, they might wish to exclude. Tone tells us how militant or how accommodating democratic movements might be, whether they are themselves open to be included in the decision-making process, or whether they view themselves as perennial outsiders. This is the issue of cooperation and co-optation, an issue that we take up in some detail in chapters 6 and 7. However, tone is not always arrived at in a consciously deliberative way but often arises as a side effect of other decisions, and often changes during the course of an organization's engagement with others.

During the early meetings, the PED struggled with issues that would help set its tone. Sponsorship by the teachers' union was clearly announced for a while as flyers put out in the union's name and sent to union representatives would list SBDM as the prominent agenda item. Hence, for a time the tone of the union, and, perhaps more explicitly, the tone of Jerry Mann, was the tone of the PED. It was engaged in a struggle where partners one day might be antagonists the next. Jerry emphasized his belief that teachers could collaborate with administrators on site councils one day and sit across the bargaining table from them on the next day.

He also was very conscious of class and race difference, while gender issues were rarely mentioned. Teachers were part of the working class and people in the African American communities and the poor are their natural allies. He saw his mission as bringing these groups together to form a coalition that would balance the influence of those who had the time and money to make their influence felt. Jerry's tone was never belligerent, but he had a job to do and he could distinguish sharply between his natural and his sometimes allies.

The issue of tone came to a head in two events during the first year of the PED's existence. The first involved the creation and subsequent reaction to a flyer, intended to invite the community to a PED meeting. The second involved the issue of whom to include in the PED and, specifically, whether to include administrators and school board members.

At an early meeting a decision was made to write and distribute a flyer to announce the formation of the PED and invite local citizens to its meeting. The group debated whether to distribute the flyer to PTA members and some objected that the PTA was a subservient "auxiliary" of the school that might swamp minority parents who already feel estranged, alienated, or intimidated. The flyer, which contained the phrase "reclaim ownership of our children's education," proved to be an important turning point in the group's history. It offended some members of the administration and the board, who felt that it implied that the schools had been taken over by an alien force and was calling for direct action to take them back.

The actual intent of the teacher who composed the flyer (she did it quickly and by herself) was to get the attention of parents and community members, which it did, but neither she nor the others expected the concerned response they got from the board. As the teachers backed off, explaining to members of the board that this was not meant as an attack on them, the actual tone, and indeed the control of the PED, was shifting in a subtle but important way.

This was amplified in the second tone-setting incident, a PED community meeting where Mann, Rhonda Silver, a high school teacher, and William Purcell, a primary school teacher, argued vehemently against inviting administrators and board members to attend PED meetings. They were overruled by the other people present. As a result of these two incidents a more conciliatory cooperative tone was established, and shortly thereafter, some school board members who had expressed concern about the PED became more open and two of them ultimately worked with it. Despite this shift in tone, what was never compromised was the PED's strong commitment to minority inclusion. As a teacher proclaimed at one meeting:

> We have no fixed agenda. We know what site-based should look like. We don't want white-only. We want it inclusive—democratically and racially conscious at the same time. That's all we got and all we should have.

Disappointed by the defeat at the meeting, William Purcell never returned as an active member of the PED. However, three years later, and against the opposition of almost all of the school board members, he initiated a successful movement to change the way the board was elected so as to maximize the probability of minority representation.

Early PED Meetings

There have been two kinds of PED meetings, community and task force. The latter sets the agendas of the community meetings. Everyone attending the community meetings was invited to also participate on the task force, but its meetings were invariably smaller than the community meetings.

To encourage minority parents to come, the first community meeting was held at one of the African American churches, an older wooden building located in a mixed neighborhood on the border of the main commercial area in the downtown. This site had been chosen by the task force to encourage African American citizens, who might otherwise find a public school inhospitable or intimidating, to attend. Nine white people and seven African Americans attended the very first meeting. Among this group were four teachers from the PED task force and an African American teacher who had not yet been to a Task Force meeting. The other African Americans included a school outreach worker and a local community organizer, both of whom were to join the task force, along with a leader of the Urban League, a social worker, two parents, and a representative from an organization called the Best Interests of Children.

Jerry Mann opened the meeting by saying:

> All of us are volunteers here with a commitment to seeing the school system governed in a more diverse and democratic way. The school district and the teachers' union have made a legal contractual commitment to site-based decision making during the last negotiations. Our aim? Not to make premature decisions—we're here to decide what to do next. How do we take the right amount of time to form a truly representative group? We want real folks here. We want to make sure the real folks are represented. Our agenda is open. What do we do next?

The discussion that followed raised many of the themes that the PED would continue to promote. An officer of the Urban League said that "we must begin with parent involvement." There then followed a discussion of time constraints on parents who have to work, whether employers would give parents time off, when to have meetings so that people could best attend, and whether teachers were already being asked to do too much on their own time.

Olive Mercy, an African American outreach worker at Steer School, spoke of the need for a room where parents would feel comfortable visiting the school during the school day. A white teacher said, "I have a vision of the school as a community center. There is a huge need for families to feel the school belongs to them. The schools need to become active places." Frank Johnson, the PED outreach organizer hired by the union, said: "This is the concept of the 'neighborhood school'—it's ours; we utilize it; there are recreation areas, places to wash clothing, day-care centers, etc. How can we make our schools family friendly." Olive Mercy: "We need a grassroots effort, one step and one community at a time." Teacher Adele Stein then added,

> For so long, schools have been the most racist of institutions. We have been the "gate-keepers." We are the ones who have promoted racism in the most subtle, unconscious ways. We have to look hard at ourselves, rethink, and move forward. We need to look at all aspects of schools in order to change our relations with the community.

Kareem Saleem, an African American community organizer from Ed City:

> It's a process of community education. Part of it requires going to the people and asking what they think; to exchange their thoughts in regard to their children's education. The atmosphere has to be open and receptive—which it isn't now. We must empower people, open the lines of communication—not stand in the stead of parents, but help them to speak. And we must also keep in touch with the students . . . don't think that a simple nine to five involvement is enough. Yes, as teachers your plate is already full. But if you want parents involved, if you want a family relationship among the schools, the parents and the children, then you must offer a greater involvement to them.

And an African American teacher raised the issues of overburdened mothers, especially single ones, and class.

These issues—time, comfort, commitment, and racism, along with inclusiveness and participation—provide a thematic structure for following the PED's subsequent engagement with the community and the development of its ideas on SBDM.

CHAPTER TWO

A Failed Attempt

The Setting: Ed City and Its Schools

Ed City, where our study is focused, has about thirty-five thousand inhabitants. It is a diverse but largely segregated community, with whites living mostly to the north of Beacon Street and African Americans living mostly to the south of it. Although housing is largely separate, the schools are desegregated to a considerable extent. There had been a systematic attempt to achieve a certain percentage of African American students and a certain socioeconomic balance in the elementary schools. With one exception, which we will discuss shortly, this balance has been maintained by busing African American children from the south side of the city to schools in the north. The African American population is officially set at about 11 or 12 percent but there have been complaints coming from members of that population that the real figure is closer to 17 percent. There is also a smaller Asian community (about 12 percent) and there is a scattering of Latino/a people (about 3 percent). For a number of historical reasons in addition to its size, the African American community networks, its numerous churches and secular organizations, are considerably more visible than are those of other community minorities. In addition to these groups, there is a more transient community of people from a variety of countries, usually students at a nearby university, whose children attend the public schools. There is one middle school and one high school in the district.

From the perspective of the school board and the central administration, there is a certain "looseness" to the chain of command in the school district which they refer to with some pride as the "Ed City Way." Although there might be slight variations on the definition, basically it means that people can intervene in the system when they feel the need without deferring to a rigid bureaucratic order. For example, according to the Ed City Way, a frustrated parent might call the superintendent without being told to start at the bottom and work up if need be. Thus, those at the top at least see the system as very open, flexible, and informal.

Although there is some variation in the degrees of hierarchy within each school, in general there is a lot of teacher autonomy within the classroom. In some of the schools, teachers participate collectively in making a variety of decisions for the school as a whole. In one, Steer School, teachers report that they make virtually all of the decisions with the principal never vetoing a decision made by the teachers. This is a tradition initially instituted by a reform-minded principal, Charles Accord, who spent twenty years at the school, 1973 to 1993.

While the school board and administration see a great deal of openness, this view is not universally held, and members of the African American community sometimes feel the need for collective action to get the board's attention. For example, in recent years, after the failure to renew the contracts of two African Americans, one a teacher and one a principal, more than a hundred African American community members marched to a school board meeting and demanded an explanation for the firing and for the underrepresentation of African Americans among teachers and administrators in the district.

Although Ed City is a relatively well-off community in comparison to many around the nation, it has a limited property tax base and high tax rates when compared to its closest neighbor, Hopsville. For example, in 1994 Hopsville's aggregate tax rate was about 8.0 while Ed City's was almost 8.9. Yet because of its greater industrial base, in Hopsville the yield per student from taxes was $3,455 whereas in Ed City it was only $2,687. This difference adds a significant but often invisible stress on the school district and the people who represent it. As property in the neighboring town becomes more attractive because of lower taxes, more people in this relatively mobile area are inclined to choose to live there, thus threatening the tax base even more. This can make it rough on teachers and support staff as well, who worry about job cuts. Moreover, the stresses on resources have led more parents to exit the schools and to choose an ever-growing number of private schools for their children. In recent years one private school was opened by parents who were concerned that their school, one with a strong academic reputation, was not offering enough for "gifted" children. Another was opened by an African American minister who felt that the schools were slighting children from that community.

Ed City has a clearly demarcated African American area where the inhabitants tend to be poor. Many people living here feel particularly alienated from the school system. Since there is a university in Ed City, there is an academic community that prizes education and attends to it, and property values are significantly determined by the reputation of schools. The value of the real estate around one of these schools, the Steer School, is considerably inflated because of its location, within walking distance from the university, and the high academic reputation of the school.

The school board has been elected on a district-wide basis and often dominated by people living within the Steer School district. A disproportionate number of the people elected to the school board either work at the university or are spouses of people who do, and there have been times when almost all of the representatives lived within a few blocks of each other in the Steer School neighborhood. There is also a professional class of relatively affluent people who have received higher education. Perhaps in contrast to the national norm and certainly to the history of school boards,[1] the business people often do not have representation on board and have not dominated it since the 1960s. This does not, of course, mean that they are not without influence on the schools, especially in the context of a tax base that is not keeping pace with its neighbor.

Despite attempts to achieve some kind of racial and class mixture through busing, as we shall see farther on, the students themselves see certain schools catering to certain social classes. All of these students come together for the first time at the single middle school, and they remain together through the single high school. Most of the more severe problems in the district arise in the two higher level schools, both because of the age of the students and because they are more characteristic of the mosaic of U.S. society than any of the elementary schools individually.

A New Superintendent Bears the "Gift" of Democracy

In 1989, James Fox, or Jimmy as everyone called him, was appointed superintendent. Jimmy was not, like the previous superintendent, a one stop administrator. He had come to Ed City in 1989 after holding four other positions, all in different states, and was gone by 1992. When we finally tracked him down on the phone, a few years and a couple of positions later, he was still eager to talk about his favorite topic,

---

1. See chapter 1.

Site-Based Decison Making (SBDM). In his own eyes he is a kind of
Johnny Appleseed spreading the idea of SBDM from one school district
to the next. As he describes himself:

> I always assumed that as superintendent I will not be there very
> long. It's always been my kind of style to put things in place that
> will remain and stay, and its their system . . . If it's good enough
> it'll stay. It'll stick.

In the eyes of his detractors, and there seem to be many, he is an
ineffective Julius Caesar, a dictator unable to prepare the ground for the
idea that he wants so badly to promote. As one former administrator put
it: "Anyone would be willing to get rid of him. He talked the game and
played it exactly the opposite. His notion was that other people ought to
give up decision-making power but not him."

When we finally located him in 1995, he was surprised that SBDM,
which seemed to him to be moving along so well when he left, had never
taken root in Ed City. Whatever the "right" description may be, Fox did
mobilize much of the community around the idea of SBDM and, not
long after he was gone, his efforts were abandoned. Few at that time were
interested in resuscitating the idea.

So when the Project for Educational Democracy (PED) began to
explore SBDM a few years later it was as if they were breaking new
ground. Most people that we have talked to explain the failure of Fox's
attempt to leave a legacy of SBDM in personal terms. Fox just left a
strong distaste in people's mouths, some tell us, and as one person, a
member of the board at that time, put it, when the dictator was gone, so
was his idea. Yet this is not completely accurate. Some of his other ideas,
for example changes in technology, took hold. So why was his conception of SBDM so difficult to hold on to?

Of course, personality plays a part in this story. It is hard to accept
an idea if its bearer contradicts it in his own relationships, as many felt
Fox did. Like the parent who tells the child I love you while pushing her
away, SBDM is not easy to accept if you feel that you are being ordered or
manipulated to adopt it.

Yet the concept of SBDM, in its very openness, lends itself to this
problem. Someone has to initiate the idea and mobilize the community
around it. Every initiation, every mobilization, every administrative edict
is a closing off as well as an opening, and it is a closing off that has someone's name attached to it. While personality may be a critical factor in
this case, it is not hard for some implementations of SBDM to gain an
aura of manipulation. Participatory democracy is a hard row to hoe if all

concerns about manipulation by interested parties are to be allayed. And with an idea as vague as SBDM, where many interpretations can be advanced as the right one, anyone in a position to embody the idea in an administrative package that says first we will do this and then that, and by "we" *I* mean, etc., has a difficult line to hold. If, in addition, the person implementing the idea is perceived as insensitive or manipulative in other respects, it will be difficult to maintain the spirit the implementation requires after that person is gone.

We remain open about why Fox left, why SBDM was forgotten, who was right and who was wrong, or whether there even was a right and *a* wrong, although many in the community have certainly formed strong views about this, or at least so it seemed to us in our individual interviews. However, to analyze this failure is to raise some of the issues that SBDM brings to the floor about democracy in its participatory form. Of course, memories are now frayed, interpretations of this episode vary, most people who rendered a judgment did not volunteer to offer an account of the personal details of the situation and we did not see the need to ask them for such. We want to get enough of the story out to compare and contrast it with the newer effort and to understand the different guises of SBDM and of democracy in its participatory form. Briefly, here is what happened as far as we know.

Fox was appointed in 1989, with a clear commitment to SBDM, after the long tenure of a well-liked but rather compliant superintendent who is described as having carried out the board's will. In contrast, Fox had a number of strong ideas, of which SBDM was right at the top.

Shortly after his arrival, Fox conceived of an elaborate project for developing long-range goals for the schools. Although it is not necessary to describe all of the details, a few are necessary to get a sense of the way he attempted to involve members of the community in his projects, and how the initial idea of SBDM was conceived.

The evolution of the idea for SBDM involved three layers of committees, one to recommend names for a "planning team" that would meet for about a year to discuss long-term goals, one of which would become the idea of SBDM. This culminated in a retreat (financially supported by local businesses) and the formation of different task forces, one to address each of the goals, including SBDM. The structure, as Byzantine as it might seem to those expecting administrators to decide matters for themselves and then to be accountable for their decisions, actually represented Fox's philosophy to involve the community from the beginning. The retreat was held in August 1990 and it developed a strategic plan for the schools.

The committees were composed of a combination of community members and people from the school system. For example, one member of the school board was on the naming committee, which was chaired by a parent. The planning team had twenty-five members and was racially mixed; of the twenty-five team members five were black (four African American and one African), one Asian American, and the rest white. Eight people were parents, one was a high school student, the others were teachers or administrators from Ed City. The team came up with goals for eight different areas: communication, finance, marketing, legislation, recognition, technology, outcomes, and SBDM. Task forces that included parents, community people, teachers, and administrators were then set up to work on each area. Their job was to set up proposals that would be presented to the board and, if passed, implemented by the administration.

The SBDM committee had a total of fourteen people on it, including Charles Accord, the principal who had established a strong consensual model of decision making in his school. It also had an assistant principal of the middle school, who was the one African American on this task force. In April 1991 the task force submitted a two-page document written by Accord and George Frank, a parent and future school board member, proposing that SBDM be implemented in the schools. The document was incorporated into the strategic plan that was presented by the superintendent to the board, which agreed to study it. Fox submitted a policy statement based on the plan, and as far as SBDM is concerned, nothing happened. However, on another front much was going on and even before the plan had been submitted to the board, Fox was told that his contract would not be renewed. He left Ed City with, seemingly, few people unhappy to see him go, including the authors of the SBDM part of the strategic plan. With Fox gone, SBDM was dead, and the resurrection needed a few years to occur.

Analysis

Why was SBDM forgotten immediately after Fox left? Was it just that, as the school board member suggested, when the dictator left, so did his idea? There were many people attracted to SBDM besides the former superintendent, and if the idea was a good one, one would have expected at least some struggle to maintain it. Yet we have heard of no such struggle and the two people who wrote the SBDM part of the strategic plan refused to rewrite it when Fox himself asked them to do so. We want to address this question, not in terms of personalities or of politics, but in terms of the idea of SBDM, the openness of the concept and what it might mean to different people.

Personality and ideas often intermingle, but a personality difference is often formed around a conceptual ambiguity and it is this that we want to explore in the remainder of this chapter. We mentioned the potential contradiction in the goal that SBDM seeks to achieve and the process through which it might be introduced. Yet when we look over the formal process by which this idea was developed, a committee of citizens naming a planning committee that formulates goals and then another citizens' committee working to implement them, it is hard to detect problems with the process at this stage, at least from the point of view of community participation. Certainly the composition of the planning committee suggests a sensitivity to racial issues. Indeed, the problem as far as we can locate it occurred elsewhere, in a certain conceptual ambiguity that SBDM allows, and that can lead to very different understandings of the idea. Consider what Fox says about his own efforts and the way he understands what he was doing in retreat.

> You know if you're a believer, if you believe in empowerment and you believe that people will make the right kinds of decisions and those decisions are right for students even though sometimes you may not have done it exactly the same way, you buy into that because you're part of the process. Now one thing you need to know about that retreat. I was not, as a superintendent, a participant in the dialogue. I was the facilitator in helping build that plan. So the community people who were there built the plan. Now that is very difficult, I think, for a superintendent to stay out of it. So there were a lot of side bar conversations going on during the retreat but that's the only real input I ever had into that plan.

> So the schools don't belong to principals, they don't belong to teachers, they belong to, you know, the taxpayers. And taxpayers are everybody, except maybe students. They would be students' parents and grandparents and that type of thing. So I think you can give power away and you gain power. It is much easier to manage a top-down controlled system. However as superintendent, I will never say site-based management is easy as far as implementation because you're allowing people to make decisions differently and those decisions sometimes look different.

In districts where I've been the superintendent in developing policies around site-based shared decision making, I have always attempted to maintain some of the controls that are necessary to assure students they're getting a quality education . . . . So I'm not one who would give the power of curriculum away . . . . Now when it comes to instructional delivery, I'd give that one away.

The language here is critical. He would "*allow* people to make decisions differently." He would not "*give* away" curriculum, but he would give away instruction. He would "allow" and he would "give" even though earlier he emphatically affirmed that the schools do not belong to him. They belong to the people. But he will now decide what and what not to give them. If they do not belong to him in the first place, then just what is he allowing and just what is he giving away? Different conceptions of education and different conceptions of democracy will give different answers to this question.

We have been told by Accord and Frank separately that when Fox got hold of the document that they wrote for the committee and developed it into a policy statement, the spirit of the document was changed. Accord says that the committee wanted powers now housed in the school board to be granted to the individual buildings, and both report that it also wanted each building to have the freedom to design the decision-making process for itself. However, the committee objected because Fox filled in all the details himself, dotted all the i's and crossed all the t's.

Having read both documents, we find some truth in this. The team's report speaks of the board and the administration delegating "real decisions within their legal limitation, to the school sites." Fox's rewrite speaks of SBDM as a strategy that actively involves parents and others outside the school. The team's document speaks of school councils formulating policy regarding curriculum, delivery system, and personnel, whereas Fox's report speaks of a council recommendation and a district-wide review. The team's report speaks of the councils' involvement in the hiring of building principals; Fox's rewrite grants authorization for members of councils to serve on screening committees, and goes somewhat further by authorizing council representation on the screening and interview committees for top district-wide administrators.

Perhaps the greatest difference is that the team's document notes that teachers would be "an excellent source for identifying potential council members from the traditionally under-represented populations," whereas Fox, while silent about underrepresented populations, proposes that council members shall be selected by their representative groups. Yet neither this difference alone, nor the fact that the implementation document was more detailed than the policy document, was sufficient reason in our minds to precipitate the break that occurred. Was there something else going on here?

We speculate that there are two different constituencies that people have in mind when SBDM is raised. One is the underrepresented minority population that is the PED's concern, and the other is those with financial means, and especially the business community, which is so important to the financial health of a school district. Although decision makers may often have both communities in mind, one or the other may take precedence given the circumstances at the time. We believe that there was a break between the SBDM proposed by Fox and the SBDM later advanced by PED. We also believe that the dispute between Fox on the one side and Accord and Frank on the other foreshadowed these different moments in Ed City's move toward SBDM later in the 1990s.

Recall that the 1980s were not especially good years for schools. And Ed City was no exception. In 1988, the *Ed City Journal* declared a projected $1,000,000 deficit out of a $26,000,000 budget. In 1989, a $1,450,000 deficit was projected, and in 1990, a $1,600,000 one was predicted. In 1989, the Ed City property tax was reported by the *Ed City Journal* (13 March 1989) to be $8.26 per hundred dollars compared to $7.13 for its neighbor. Schools took up more than half of that amount.

Ed City often seems to be operating at the edge of its financial resources. There were years when, because state law required early notification of layoffs and because the state legislature could never agree on funding until the last minute, the school board had to fire all untenured teachers and even some tenured ones. Usually it hired them back when the board found that it could scrape up the money to pay them.

The tax base was threatened, as businesses closed in the downtown area and competition from retail establishments in Hopsville, the community to the north, drained customers from the Roosevelt Shopping Mall. Roosevelt had been built in the 1960s and served for a while as the region's most popular shopping center until the Interstate was built along the northern side of Hopsville rather than the southern border of Ed City. That highway brought with it an enormous commercial area for Hopsville. While Ed City retained its charm, Hopsville, not without charm itself, was raking in the money. First, the popular Italian restaurant in Roosevelt Mall in Ed City closed, then the furniture store, and then the upscale department store chain was replaced by a downscale chain. While in no sense a depressed area, as school began in 1991 the *Ed City Journal*, reporting on a survey performed on assessed property valuation per child, noted that Hopsville's assessed valuation per child was

$71,000 whereas the figure in Ed City was $52,000 and salaries were behind those of other, comparable school districts by almost $4,000.

The SBDM that Fox envisaged was most likely a response to these conditions. That the retreat was financed by major local businesses, including the most prominent local bank in the area, was probably more than just a short-run response to a tightening budget. It was a way to connect the business community to the long-term problems of the schools, including their financial problems. The support for the retreat, albeit rather small change, was one sign of what an alliance might effect.

The appeal to business is apparent in Fox's implementation document. It lists businesses as a separate representative body; thus "Council membership shall be equally divided between representative staff members and community (parents, businesses, non-parent) members," as if business people were a category unto themselves, neither parents nor non-parents. Although there is also an appeal for gender, ethnic, and other forms of representative equity, there is no similar listing for other interest groups such as labor, environmental activists, civil rights organizations, or social service agencies. The vagueness of the selection procedure, the overlap between business people and parents and business people and non-parents, makes this a difficult document to understand without reference to the financial needs of the district. A system that is viewed as attractive and open to business attracts more business and has a potential for more revenue.

George Frank, the coauthor with Accord of the original plan, tells us that Fox was very responsive to the business community, meeting regularly with the Chamber of Commerce and the leaders of the most prominent local bank in the area. Perhaps most significantly, after the site-based proposal was written, Fox, along with a principal, a teacher, a school board member, and a parent, was sent to a national meeting of school administrators. While they were there, Fox told the others that he had arranged a meeting with representatives of a Fortune 500 corporation that had developed a plan for site-based management of schools and was looking for districts to adopt it.

Frank, along with the president of the teachers' union, attended the meeting. Frank said that the company plan met with considerable disfavor from both of them. He recalls that the attitude of the company representative was: "We're a successful business; we know how to run a school district and we will guarantee results if you do what we tell you to do." Frank felt that values that he and others in the community cared about, equity and inclusiveness, were not concerns of the corporation. He described the scene in the room after the company representatives left as tense. Fox tried to sell the plan and was met with silence. Frank then took the material that the company had handed out, ripped it up, and threatened to run for the board. At our interview, about seven years after this meeting, he noted that only a few days before this interview the company had announced the layoff of fifteen thousand workers, which was to him an obvious sign that it was not as competent as Fox thought.

Fox's appeal to business was in keeping with the increasing national influence of business over public education nationally, a move that was expressed by various national documents on school reform.[2] Accord may be correct in his concern that Fox was giving away everyone's power but his own. Yet the effect of Fox's rhetoric leaves an impression that he wanted to reduce the distance between professional authority and economic power in a climate in which school budgets were unstable.

Other Goals of SBDM

Although SBDM may serve to strengthen links to the financial community in a time of economic uncertainty, this is not its only possible use. Steer School Principal Accord used it to affirm the professional jurisdiction of teachers by establishing a consensual form of decision making in which teachers had significant jurisdiction over matters that are usually decided by the principal alone. His model largely was confined to the body of teachers and administrators in his school, with parents serving on advisory bodies upon invitation and at the pleasure of the professional staff. It had the effect of strengthening the cohesion of a professional body and unifying the building's administrator and the building's teachers. Here the professional authority of teachers was reinforced by the principal, who refused to veto decisions that had been agreed upon by the teachers' consensual process. As Accord described the Team document in similar terms:

> We originally designed it to strongly suggest that at every building level there needed to be a participatory decision-making process, you know, to involve all of the constituencies . . . . We did not spell it out in terms of specifics. What we spelled out was that the principal would not have veto power once this body made decisions.

---

2. See, for example, *A Nation at Risk: The Imperative for Educational Reform,* A Report to the Nation and the Secretary of Education, U.S. Department of Education, by the National Commission on Excellence in Education, April 1983.

Parents and community members did not have equal status with teachers and administrators. Rather, they were invited to participate on specific projects. They were not members of a permanent decision-making body, nor was there a mechanism to enable them to select their own representatives. We do not know whether Accord was willing to give up the authority to decide when it is appropriate for people from outside of the professional staff to serve on decision making bodies or whether he would have been willing to give up the authority to determine who should serve. His document suggests that he would, but his concern that Fox was dictating a uniform model for all schools suggests that these issues were not resolved in his own mind.

In any event the document that Accord coauthored for the team has no hint that the inclusion of business was a prominent factor. Indeed, a number of people on the team were active in the union and one was head of an advocacy group that frequently came into conflict with one of the largest businesses in town. His group would organize Christmas carolers to sing in front of the business and would take considerable delight in changing words of the songs to highlight any Scrooge-like features of the enterprise. The enterprise also happened to be one of the sponsors of Fox's retreat.

The comment about the need to include "underrepresented" populations on the council represents a strong background consideration held by many of the members of this group, and should be distinguished both from Fox's concern to find allies in the business community for the schools and even from the model practiced in Accord's school, which advanced professionalism and in which parents sometimes served as invited participants.

Until the PED was formed, Fox's proposal for SBDM had been essentially tabled by the school board and ignored. Both policy and personality became intermingled in the minds of many who saw Fox as heavy-handed or manipulative, and the taste in the mouths of the participants was so bad, one of our interviewees told us, that even those who had been very much in favor of SBDM seemed not to have the heart to push it.

The Resurgence of SBDM

SBDM had to wait until 1994 to resurface when a combination of factors converged to bring it to the attention of the community. First, as a student Jerry Mann had gone to Yugoslavia to research worker decision making in Yugoslav factories. He had been active in nonunion associations that advanced the participatory idea and he was eager to advance it within organized labor. Although he had not played an active role in the process set in place by the superintendent in 1990, he was supportive of the idea of SBDM. Four years later, at a time when both public schools and teachers' unions were being attacked by Republican governors and Republican-controlled legislatures[3] and public confidence in the schools was in steep decline, unions at the national level were encouraging their locals to explore nonadversarial modes of decision making.

Although Mann and some of the teachers were ready to move, and while the coauthor (with Accord) of the SBDM team's proposal, George Frank, had now been elected to the board, it took a painful catalytic event to bring about the renewed interest. This was the breakdown of negotiations with the school board and a very bitter strike just before the beginning of the 1994 school year. When a contract was finally agreed upon and signed, the teachers submitted a letter of understanding, which both they and the board signed. It read:

> The [union] and the Board agree that as a district we need to summarize the practice and procedures of site based decision making across the district and develop philosophy [sic] that reflects our mission and strategic plan. Therefore, during the 1996–97 school year, a district-wide committee shall be formed with full representation of faculty, staff, administration, students, parents and community to meet the above agreement.

At the time, this letter of understanding was interpreted in different ways. One person who helped negotiate the contract for the board, himself an advocate of SBDM, told us that he felt the board accepted the letter and the creation of a study committee simply to stonewall the issue. Since the letter required no legal or moral commitment to implement SBDM, he told us that members of the board probably felt there

---

3. A spokesperson for Governor John Engler, the Republican governor of Michigan, is quoted as saying:

> The union used to run the show in this state. The Michigan Education Association was probably the most powerful education union in the country until the Republicans took control. Now Governor Engler has predicted that within 10 years there will be no more MEA. They will be obsolete.

Peter Applebome, "GOP Efforts Put Teachers' Union on the Defensive: Reform Issues at Stake," *New York Times*, 4 September 1995, 1:7.

was no harm in creating a study committee, hoping that "it'll study it to death and nothing concrete will come out of it."

Whatever members of the board may have felt, the union's director Mann interpreted the letter as a binding commitment to implement SBDM. He began a process to prepare for that 1996–1997 year when the district-wide committee would be in place, and to give flesh to the vague skeleton provided in the letter.

The local union began by making a commitment to include often-excluded groups in the process and it obtained funds from its statewide organization to bring in Frank Johnson, the African American organizer who had considerable experience in other African American communities. It was felt that if the African American community, and then other excluded communities as well, were not mobilized, the parent and community representation aspect of SBDM would fall to people who had leisure, money, and higher education—in other words, the usual school participants. Johnson immediately began making contacts within the African American community as well as trying to reach out to the less numerous Latinos and Southeast Asians.

Next, Mann addressed a meeting of union representatives in the various schools. It was a brief presentation in which he committed himself and the union to move ahead with the project. He did not ask for a vote, but told them that a task force would be formed and invited them to participate. In December 1994, seven teachers who were union representatives met with the director and the African American organizer. The director distributed a three-year schedule for bringing SBDM making to the district. He entitled this: "The [union's name] 'Project for Educational Democracy' (a shared/SBDM-making task force)."

The major function of the task force has been the planning of monthly community meetings. The director of the union and the small group of teachers (at the time, all white, with the exception of Olive Mercy, the African American outreach worker at Steer School) who formed the core of the initial group, were especially concerned to use SBDM as a way to reach out to the African American community, and to involve them in the day to day work of their schools. Because of this concern, a lot of time was initially spent on planning the location of the meetings.

As we indicated in the previous chapter, the task force arranged to hold its meetings at one of the black churches on the border between an African American residential area and the downtown business district. However, after a few monthly meetings, they were moved to the public library a few blocks away and on the border of the white and business communities. The move was decided on after it became known that the minister of the church had plans to develop a private school. Another reason that has been given to us is that some members of the African American community who were not members of this church felt a bit uncomfortable attending a meeting in it. If this reason is accurate it highlights the problems that arise for even the most progressive groups, when trying to address a group of people who are similar in some ways but different in others. Later, as the PED's efforts began to involve more African Americans, members would experience some of the ideological differences that exist among African Americans about the governance of public education.

The library was not only in a different part of the city, it was also a very different space. In the church, people sat in pews and faced a single facilitator, usually Mann, standing in front of the pews—an arrangement that did not fit the PED's ideas on participation. The library room had moveable chairs and tables that could be arranged separately for small groups, or in a circle that allowed everyone to face everyone else and minimized the consciousness of a single leader. Thus, even though more distant from the African American neighborhood, the shape of the room opened up many different possibilities in this attempt to construct and enact a community. Over time, the community meetings were merged with the task force meetings and were held in the union offices.

Whatever the reason for the change, it should be noted that it was difficult to sustain the initial impulse to meet on the home turf of the members of the African American community, and eventually because the library room was sometimes booked, the meetings were moved back into the union hall.

Wherever they met, however, they maintained the same impulse, that is, to involve the community in their deliberations on site-based projects without imposing any particular conception of governance on them. They believed that democracy and education required greater participation and involvement in meaningful decision making, but they also felt that to be properly democratic, they could not impose their conception of democracy on anyone. They wanted to move ahead, but they did not want to tell anyone where to go or how to get there.

CHAPTER THREE

Engaging in Democratic Discourse Democratically

The Task Force

It was a day in late June. School had closed for the summer and four white teachers, Marcy Bright, Joyce Rogers, Jane Crew, and Adele Stein, joined Olive Mercy, the African American school outreach worker, Frank Johnson, the African American Community organizer who had been hired by the union, Kareem Saleem, an African American community activist, and union Director Jerry Mann in the offices of the Edge City Teachers' Union to plan a community meeting. This was the eighth meeting of the Project for Educational Democracy's (PED) task force. There had also been eight community meetings since the PED's inception. The first four were held in the local African American Church, the last four in the public library. The average attendance in these meetings was twenty persons. After the observers (three) and the task force members (six to eight) are subtracted from the membership at each meeting, approximately eight new persons participated in each meeting, but usually not the same eight persons.

The task force meeting on this June evening lasted three hours. Jerry Mann proposed five areas (outreach, coordination, resource facilitation, orientation of newcomers, leadership) for the task force to consider for the community meeting. However, throughout most of the meeting this agenda was ignored.

Rather, the teachers were worried about how to break the ice at that meeting. They wanted people to tell stories about their experiences with the schools. They decided that before a person could tell a story, she or he had to eat an M&M. This would be the best way to break the

37

ice. (They considered the game where a person holds an orange under the chin, as another method of breaking the ice.) They settled on M&Ms of four colors (red, yellow, green, brown). Each person was to take a handful of M&Ms, and in order to eat one, the person must first speak to a subject under the topic of that color. Before people left the meeting, they were to invite someone to lunch.

Presumably, this was to create a shared experience, and that experience would be available for people who wanted to act together. The teachers were attempting to create a mutuality of experience, an affective community that would be continued outside the space where it originated.

We want to examine the meanings of the M&Ms in this meeting, and we want to understand why breaking the ice was so important to this group. We also want to show how two agendas in this meeting, the teachers' and the director of the union's were negotiated. It is our view that in this meeting itself we encounter two different conceptions of inclusiveness and that they represent two alternative understandings of the democratic process. The teachers, trying to gain acceptance from the community for the activity that they were committed to, believed it was important to develop emotional ties between themselves and the parents and community members who came to the meeting. Jerry Mann, who believed that legitimacy had already been established through the letter of understanding between the union and the board, wanted to find an effective way to present site-based decision making (SBDM) to the community and to engage their participation. This difference, which was quickly muted by Mann's giving in to the teachers' understanding, is a faint reflection of the differences that we saw when the old superintendent wanted to deliver inclusive and participatory decision making to the school principals. In this case, however, Mann quickly sized up the contradiction, and did not press his own agenda.

How Do We Break the Ice?

Marcy opened the meeting: "This will be informal, right? How should we break the ice?" Frank suggested facetiously, "How about rum and Coke?" Jane countered,

> Oh, I know how to break the ice, I do it all the time with my kids. How about M&Ms. We bring a big bag of M&Ms, everybody takes a handful, they will be different colors. Nobody can eat an M&M until they tell something about who they are, something

special. Everybody goes around the circle and says something personal. This breaks the ice. One color can be red, another can be yellow, another green, and another brown. Red can mean education, or schools, and like that.

Adele, who arrived late because she had locked her keys in her car, immediately understood what Jane was talking about, "This is all about inclusiveness and commitment."

Marcy: What will we have people talk about?

Jerry: Why not just say what we are thinking about doing next fall, the second year of our plan?

Frank: No, this is more just getting people together.

Jane: They'll tell stories, we'll create three scenarios, depending on what color of M&M they get, they'll have to tell a story. We'll have four groups: red, blue, white, green. Each group will share its stories with the larger group.

Marcy: What scenarios?

Jane: How about one about Johnny spit on Jimmy, another one on the school calendar, and another one on your child not getting into the class she wanted to take?

Joyce: This sounds good, who will write the scenarios?

Jane: I will.

Jerry: So what are we going to do after everybody tells their story? Where would we go next? I would prefer working the crowd, more than games and ice-breakers. I like breaking down barriers by talking with people you don't know, and connecting them with people they don't know.

Adele: Jerry, we'll come back in a big circle, and a representative from each group will summarize their group stories.

Jerry: Ah, geeze. What about these questions I've got up on the wall for the whole task force?

On the wall, hanging from a large bulletin board are the following questions, which Jerry read.

Jerry: A. Ongoing outreach, and internal organizational interests;
           B. Selection and coordination of places/sites to visit;
           C. Resource facilitation—speakers, literature;
           D.Orientation pieces, statements defining site-based;
           E. Coordination and Leadership.

           Our goal is to get people coming back.

Olive: Outreach is a problem. There has been an abuse of funds. The [noncertified outreach] workers have low self-esteem. They feel like they aren't part of the district.

Kareem: This will work in three phases: information, strategic planning, and organization. We have to have visual aids. We have to use the media, and we have to use the existing organizations, like the churches.

Marcy: What's our goal?

Olive: How many years must my people suffer? We gained in the sixties and now we are losing all that we gained.

Frank: Hey guys, the sixties are over. We are into multiculturalism. The sixties didn't prepare whites for blacks, or blacks for whites.

Marcy: We have to have people tell real stories. We have to ask the tough, hard questions.

Jerry: This is risky business. We're taking big risks. We have to build a public base, there may be a power void if we democratize everything. There are big dangers. People are talking about privatizing public education, vouchers, and charter schools. Let's go back to our questions.

Marcy: A road show. We'll visit all the schools.

Jane: The next meeting? Shall we have overheads?
          We'll have big and little circles.

Jerry: Overly structured for a social event.

The above conversation brings to the fore a number of critical issues about democracy, legitimization, and the ambiguous position of the PED. On the one hand, Jerry continued here to think like a union organizer who had existing goals and strategies in mind. On the other hand, he provided a major impetus in unleashing a project the spirit of which was open ended and encouraging of community rather than union direction. Given that he held that there was already an agreement between the union and the board, he believed that the agenda should be structured so as to advance the ultimate and agreed-upon goal of instituting SBDM. Hence, he saw these meetings as largely a way to advance that program through his five-step strategic action plan. He also expressed some hesitation about, as he put it, "democratizing everything," a comment that can be read within the context of his fundamental commitment to advance the legitimacy of public education and to do so through the union. His comment suggests a concern that if such meetings became a place where people just voiced their criticisms of the public schools, they would add fuel to those who were advancing alternatives to them. At the end, he went along with the spirit of the meeting although he defined the event as a social rather than a political or educational one.

In contrast, Marcy believed that it was best to let it all hang out and to encourage people to tell their stories and to air their grievances. Perhaps aware that teachers, the union, and SBDM may have had no more legitimacy among the African American people than did the administration and the school board, she believed that rapport would be established by listening to one another's stories in an uncritical way.

Olive voiced both of these concerns. She was there because she hoped that SBDM might do something to empower the noncertified workers as well as the parents and she voiced her sense that time was working against them and things needed to be done fast. However, speed and the fullest participation do not always go together.

Skip ahead two weeks. The next community meeting was held from 7:00 to 8:45 PM in the city library. Twenty people were in attendance, eight new faces. Jane came prepared with a large bag of colored M&Ms, but for reasons that are not clear, the M&M strategy was not used. Marcy asked the group to form itself into four smaller groups. Instead of M&Ms, each group was given a large sheet of paper. Each person in the groups was asked to select a symbol that represented who they were. The groups were then asked to talk about populations that were not well represented by the city's schools. Groups were also asked to describe four ways in which the members were like other people. This took nearly the entire meeting time (from 7:15 to 8:15). The room filled with quiet, small group discussion, as members drew pictures and shared stories about what their symbols meant. A variety of symbols were presented, from gardens, to books, flowers, the globe, a life jacket, the Star of David, a fist. Each group then reported on its symbols and on the groups it felt were currently excluded, including students, parents, alumni, the police, support staff, business, booster clubs, the churches, and special-needs parents. Members of the task force and two parents agreed to attempt to make contact with these groups.

Now move ahead to a community meeting held in early September. School had begun and there were ten community members present, along with the task force. Four African American parents were present. Twenty-five chairs circled the room. Adele gave a brief history of the PED. Tonight they were going to focus on how decisions are made. She told the group that "we know change is hard to do, it takes time. It is a process. We want to look at what works and what can be changed."

Marcy stepped forward and read a short story, *The Seven Blind Mice*, by C. D. Young, to the group.

> Marcy: There are seven blind mice, they are seven different colors: red, yellow, green, gray, orange, blue, and white. The mice are crawling over an elephant. Each reports something different.

> Adele: We are trying to build a picture, everybody sees something different. How are decisions made in our schools? We want to divide into groups, based on the colored dot on your name tag: blue, red, green, white. Jane is going to read you three scenarios, and the peo-

ple in your group are going to tell stories about each scenario, and then report back to the larger group.

Jane: We have three situations: the school calendar and the hot days in school in late August; Johnny hit a teacher and what should be done; your child did not get placed in the right class.

The large group divided up into five small groups. In the first group, a mother, Pamela Stern, told the following story about her daughter:

My daughter has been a straight A student. Last spring she started getting bad grades in her math class. The teacher would call her to the front of the room to solve a math problem, and then humiliate her when she made a mistake. My daughter became very upset. I first went to see a counselor about the problem. The counselor made it clear that he did not want to confront the teacher. So, I went to the teacher who said that my daughter had to work harder. I told the teacher that I wanted to hire a tutor. The teacher said [in a discouraging way], "that will cost you sixty dollars an hour." We went to a tutor and he said my daughter was doing just fine, that she knew the material. When I was writing the check out for sixty dollars, he asked me what I was doing. I told him that the teacher had told me that this was the hourly fee for tutors. The tutor laughed and said, "Oh, no, it's twenty-five dollars." When my daughter went back to class, the teacher embarrassed her again. Maybe the teacher was irritated that I went to the counselor first. Next time I would go to the teacher first. But I did not like how this worked and I just resigned myself to the fact that it's only for one year and hope that the damage to my daughter won't be too great.

The red group reported to the larger group on the school calendar. Their spokesperson was parent Georgia Senn:

Schools have to be in session for one hundred and eighty days. I was on the calendar committee for the school board. We looked at different options: starting when—[a near-by city] starts, starting when the college starts, and we decided you could never make everybody happy. The State Board says there has to be a twelve game football season every fall. If schools start after Labor Day there is not enough time for twelve games. So the state dictates the calendar. But it doesn't make any sense. In New York State schools run an hour longer every day. We could do that. My daughter is losing out on almost a full year's education, because this district keeps to a short 189 day schedule.

Adele brought the group back together.

Adele: What do we see here, like the seven blind mice, how decisions are made is an issue of perception: who sees what. What we see is not what the school board sees. Decisions are being made all the time and the people that they effect are not always brought into the decision-making process. Next time we will talk about discipline.

The meeting ended, although without any one addressing what the school board, or, for that matter, what the teachers saw. This was clearly a meeting intended to help parents get comfortable with the process of talking about schools in the presence of teachers and not a meeting to advance the many different views of the "elephant."

The Teachers' Theory of Community

The teachers on the task force wanted SBDM to be based on a model of communal, participatory democracy. They belonged to what Sartre called a pledged group.[1] The concept of SBDM was a kind of symbol that pledged them to group unity. This pledge operated in a way that fused the teachers together in reciprocal relationships. They took turns setting up the meetings, bringing treats, snacks, and beverages. They divided up responsibilities, all in a joint effort to move the project forward. The teachers at this time were united against the school board's conception of representative democracy and frequently they talked about SBDM as an alternative to it. Although the board is made up of elected citizens, the teachers felt the board was unresponsive to the needs of teachers, students, families, and minority and poor communities. Hence, two models of democracy (participatory and representative) clashed in the teacher's minds. This conflict unified their project. They

---

1. Jean-Paul Sartre, *Critique of Dialectical Reason,* trans. Alan Sheridan-Smith (London: Verso/NLB, 1976), 417–444.

were single minded in their focus. They wanted shared decision making in the schools, and they wanted the schools to meet the needs of all students, from all of the different communities that made up the community served by the district. And, they were especially interested in the African American community, because they believed that the concerns of its members had often been neglected.

This was the problem. The teachers had a theory about how to create community through mutual sharing. This concept then led to a theory about how to make the schools better—bring the community into the schools! However, they did not want to impose this concept of community on others. They wanted people to create this concept together, in the meetings the teachers were sponsoring. This was the teachers' project, local community co-performed in the PED meetings.

The people from the community who came to the meetings did not share this vision, at least initially. They did not know about the teachers' theory of community. They did not understand what SBDM was (and the teacher's wouldn't tell them, because this would have been imposing a definition). The community members were not joined together into a fused and pledged group, as the teachers were. Consequently, the teachers' theory did not specify how one moved from one meeting to the next, other than to recreate a new situational community in the next meeting. There was no transcendent project.

Then what was going on here? In both community meetings teachers were using their pedagogical skills to produce interactions which created community solidarity. They were putting their version of democratic decision making into practice. At the same time the public was cooperating. Adults willingly sat and listened to Marcy read *The Seven Blind Mice*. Adults willingly took name tags with different colored dots and assembled themselves into small groups. Once in the groups, these community members were ready to tell stories about the three scenarios. These stories connected a personal difficulty or problem the parent had encountered with the school, a public institution. In this connection, the private and public sides of everyday life were joined. More importantly, the teachers succeeded in bringing the issue of the decision-making process back into the private life of the parent and the child.

By focusing on how decisions are made, but not on SBDM, the teachers opened up the very discourse they wanted SBDM to address. That is, they showed this group of parents how the PED connected to the private troubles parents experience with their children, as their children go through the school system.

This connection has been forged through the use of everyday performance techniques teachers use when they mobilize their classes for instructional purposes. These techniques create the conditions for an empathetic sharing of experiences. The value of these stories was rooted in the concrete experiences that the parents had in dealing with the schools. The teachers then connected these stories to the larger decision-making structure that operated in the schools.

This is why things such as M&Ms, colored name tags, and identity symbols are so important. Breaking the ice is equivalent to opening the doors to a community conversation, it is a way of finding a common ground for a shared experience. Breaking ice creates a space that community members can enter. In sharing name tags, life symbols, and stories about the schools, the community members come together in a form of discourse that is not otherwise made available by the school. There is no space for these kinds of conversations in the monthly school board meetings. The PTA is also not a site where this kind of talk can occur. The PED has created a new space for a public conversation about education in Edge City.

Conclusion

Not wanting to impose a definition on others for fear that this would be undemocratic, the planning group was caught in the paradoxical situation of needing to construct a democratic community when they feared that the very process of "constructing" a community was itself undemocratic. At these moments they sought a conception of democracy that preceded the community they wanted to create. This conception sought, through ice breakers and party games, to break down the differences between individuals, differences presumably tied to race, class, and professional position. This process of breaking down barriers produced a shared experience, out of which the members of the PED intended to create a democratic community, however temporary it might have been. On the other hand, there was work to be done, meetings to be planned, people to invite, issues to be defined, agendas to be developed, all those things that concerned Jerry Mann and, incidentally, that had also concerned Superintendent Jimmy Fox earlier. All of this required a division of labor that might work against the communal or participatory conception of authority.

Before we examine the way in which this tension was expressed in the subsequent working relationships of the PED with the established school authorities, we want to explore one of the major reasons why the value of community is so important to its members. For this, we need to examine the recent history of race relations in Ed City and its schools.

CHAPTER FOUR

Race and School in Ed City

When I was a schoolboy we threw rocks and epithets at every Negro kid in range . . . I want something better for my children.
—*Ed City white parent, 1967*

Negroes are dying in Vietnam, yet you wish to impose a position of inequality in education and employment. Search your conscience.
—*Ed City African American minister, 1967*

I have no shame whatsoever that my skin is dark . . . I'm rather proud of it . . . [but] I am trying to look at the problem from the white man's point of view . . . "What are you afraid of?"
—*Letter to the editor, Ed City African American mother, 10 October 1963*

Introduction: The Concept of an "Underrepresented Minority"

If the term *Ed City Way* mobilizes the school board and the administration, the concern with exclusion, which we translate as a concern for "underrepresented minorities," mobilizes the Project for Educational Democracy (PED) and its friends. At least since the Civil Rights movement in the United States, the conception of minority "underrepresentation" is so common that only the most conservative members of the community might question the assumptions about representation that it entails, believing either that the term is redundant because it simply refers to those who have lost an election, or that it is empty because individuals, not groups, are represented. Yet no one points this out, and while the members of the Ed City school board have varying degrees of sensitivity to the issue even the most conservative member expressed embarrassment to us when noting the absence of African Americans on the current board.

Yet, to push the conservative point of view for a moment, just what does it mean for a minority to be excluded or underrepresented in a system where anyone who chooses to run gets on the ballot, where everyone is allowed to vote, and where those who receive the majority of the votes are elected to office? This question is, of course, intended to raise the issue of what counts as "representation" in a noncorrupt system (which we believe Ed City to be) where, nevertheless, elections result in the systematic exclusion of certain groups. In this chapter we want to explore the issue in terms of the history of recent race relations in Ed City schools and the way in which that history contributes to distrust and immobility around issues of race in the present.

The Ed City school board is a representative body, and until 1999 each member was voted in by the community as a whole. Thus, every member was, at least theoretically, accountable to everyone in the community. Those who supported this system, as opposed to election by wards or districts, believed that an at-large system encourages members to address the interest of the community as a whole rather than any one individual district or school within it.

Members of the school board are not paid for their services, and unlike some other offices, school board membership is not generally seen as a springboard to other political opportunities. There are few, if any, real perks that come with the job, a lot of responsibility, many demands, and for some a lot of soul searching and headaches.

It is a civic duty that is not particularly attractive to many people in the community. Membership is a time-consuming matter, with two public meetings a month usually lasting at least two hours each, many additional committee meetings, and visits to individual schools. Moreover, given a certain level of informality, which we described in chapter 2 as the Ed City Way, school board members attempt to be available to dissatisfied teachers and parents.

Hard work and good intentions of the school board notwithstanding, members of the PED believe that both formal and informal avenues of influencing school governance remain closed to the five thousand African Americans and to poor people within the school district. While class issues have entered into the discussions periodically, indeed usually raised by African American participants in the PED, early on in our study the key leaders of the PED argued that their project is all about race. One teacher put it this way:

> The schools will be the place where race issues are confronted, if
> they are ever to be confronted by this community. We want the

school to be a safe place for these conversations to occur. (Interview, 20 January 1995)

"Underrepresented minority" can mean two things. First, it can refer to a system that results in a group's being systematically excluded from key policy- and decision-making positions, and second, it can refer to the effect that this exclusion has on children from certain groups in the schools. A lot of people do not believe that these two meanings necessarily go together. That is, they question whether the assumption that the conjunction entails is valid. They do not see why elected individuals from any group are not able to make good decisions for children from all groups, nor are they willing to accept the idea that the best educational decisions for children from one group will necessarily come from adults that are members of that same group. We discuss the logic of the conjunction in a later chapter, but here we want to show why these assumptions have credibility for members of the PED as well as for many in the African American Community in Ed City.

The question that we asked about the possibility of underrepresentation in a noncorrupt system where anyone can run and anyone can vote is intended to open up the question of whether democratic forms of government should be concerned about groups at all or whether it is necessary to reject group politics at the formal level of representation. In a later chapter we address this issue in terms of larger theoretical frameworks and explore alternative conceptions of representation, alternatives that take into account group differences. Our study strongly suggests that under certain conditions and in certain settings group considerations need to be taken into account.

In this chapter, we want to show some of the ways in which underrepresentation matters in determining the relationship between the African American population and the Ed City school system. We begin by filling out the two positions about representation as we find them in this community. These alternative positions are not restricted to Ed City, but are played out every day on the national scene.

Two Views of Representation

The first is the view that people should relate to political institutions as individuals who work to put aside their prejudices and try to judge each issue on its own merits. It is thought that when the final judgment is in, race or social class or religion should have as little bearing on the results as possible. Certainly people have biases, but in running for office on a community-wide basis, and in inviting citizen input, the bias will be minimized and judgment will come close to approximating the best interests of the community and its children. Hence, what we should strive for is a race-neutral policy where everyone can see as far as possible the consequences of a course of action for all the children in the community. Indeed, many argue that this was the very essence of the Civil Rights movement—to remove the restrictions placed on individuals because of their membership in groups.

The logic of the above point of view should lead to a rejection of the very conception of "underrepresentation." If the procedures are open, that is, if everyone can run for office and everyone can vote, then the political will has been satisfied. Although no one takes the logic quite this far, we will see in later chapters that there is a very strong connection in the minds of key members on the board between a community-wide, race-neutral election and the best educational decisions for the children as a whole.

The alternative view speaks to a history of race relations in which racial issues have always been a factor in American political and educational life and continue to be so. According to this view, to fail to take into account race in the very selection of the decision makers and in the evaluation of the decisions is to continue to be conveniently blind to the way in which race serves as a signal for the distribution of privileges and burdens. Hence, from this point of view, race relations in this country are inhibited because the race-neutral ideal expressed above rests on a race-neutral history that is false. This official history, when it contributes to continuing patterns of exclusion and rejection, contributes to feelings of betrayal and mistrust in the African American community.

Forgetting is seen as a critical part of the first view; remembering is a critical part of the second. The first does not take into account the reservoir of rebuffs and rejections that many African Americans have experienced. It is this habit of forgetting that leaves the mostly white political and educational leadership with a history that is cut off from that of the African American community. It ignores their repeated experiences of rebuffs and disappointments.

More specifically, this view observes that a subtle, two-layer system of racial forgetting perpetuates America's reluctance to enact a thoroughgoing system of racial equality. In this forgetting people are viewed as simply individuals rather than as individuals who are also members of different races. Hence, once this forgetting is in place, to look for systematic inequalities along racial lines seems almost un-American, a view that accounts for the backlash against affirmative action, for example, on the national level.

At the community and national levels, the habit of forgetting controls what passes as official racial history: sacred, ritual remembrances of the past.[1] It manipulates and shapes this history by controlling how race is named, defined, and honored officially. This system refuses even to recognize race as an issue in situations obviously defined by racial politics.

Arguments such as the above lie behind the concept of "underrepresented," and are at the basis of the reform impulse the PED represents. This is a historical argument about how the past continues to influence or to be repeated in the present. However, it assumes an important conceptual point, that is, that for some political and educational purposes it is appropriate to treat people as part of a group and to address representation from the group as well as the individual standpoint.

In this chapter we want to address both of these. We want to show why the concept of underrepresented minority is an appropriate one for addressing the problems of some people, and then we want to show that the concept fits much of the historical experience of African Americans in Ed City. We do not address the logic of the conjunction of the two questions, reserving that for a later chapter. However, we show how without representation events of historical significance are forgotten while their meaning is still relived in the experience of people.

On the Concept of Underrepresentation

There is considerable credibility to the view that wants to treat representation as an affair of the individual and to avoid reifying group membership. First, while a person may be identified as belonging to a group, she may not herself feel that particular group membership to be primary. She may want to highlight another aspect of her identity. Second, it is hard to know where to draw the line and say that this is one group and this is another. For example, should people with Asian background all be treated as one group or should they be treated as people with Indian, Pakistani, Chinese, Japanese, and Korean backgrounds. Thirdly, it does not seem reasonable to think of all groups as entitled to

---

1. Here is a contemporary case in point: two years ago Ed City's Historical Society invited a group of elderly African Americans to contribute to the Society's archive. The local university's program in African American studies sponsored a public event where this new archive was discussed and presented to the community. The *Ed City Journal* waited three weeks to report this event in a short story that neglected to report on the public ceremony and its ritual significance for the African American community.

representation. What reason is there for Cuban Americans or Hungarian or Russian Americans to have separate representatives? Fourth, groups are usually not monolithic and people of the same group can see their interests differently. Finally, it could be argued there is a perfectly reasonable mechanism for any group that wishes to achieve representation to do so, and that is to convince as many members of the group as possible to vote for a certain candidate. And, if there are not enough voters within the group to win, then one must convince enough people outside the group that it is to their material or ideological advantage to vote for that candidate. This is the interest-aggregating tradition of American politics and it has worked well for some people. These arguments suggest not, however, that the concept of underrepresentation is incoherent or inappropriate, but that it needs to be applied to appropriate groups.

What Is an Underrepresented Group?

Iris Young has a useful although not completely adequate definition of a group. She says that

[a] social group is a collective of persons differentiated from at least one other group by cultural forms, practices, or way of life. Members of a group have a specific affinity with one another because of their similar experience or way of life, which prompts them to associate with one another more than with those not identified with the group, or in a different way. . . . Group identification arises . . . in the encounter and interaction between social collectivities that experience some differences in their way of life and forms of association, even if they also regard themselves as belonging to the same society.[2]

We want to adopt this definition for the sake of the discussion below, but we also want to note the fluidity that often characterizes groups, and to view cultural forms, practices and ways of life not as containers that hold individuals, but as constituting webs of meaning and significance that people share to varying degrees with one another and that affect their social and political interactions. Group membership is

---

2. Iris Marion Young, *Justice and the Politics of Difference,* (Princeton: Princeton University Press, 1990), 43. We see our addition as consistent with Young's rejection of groups as having an essential nature.

thus not an essential quality but it describes nodes of intelligibility and fellow feeling that for some are quite thick and that for others thin out as their involvement as equals with members of groups with different nodes of experience and intelligibility increases. What we want to suggest about the concept of "underrepresented group" is that it is the curtailment of this involvement as equals that constitutes underrepresentation and that underrepresentation is a problem when it tracks to historical experiences and present conditions that maintain these unequal relations.

African Americans are "underrepresented" in Ed City not just because they often are not present on the school board—in fact over the years there has sometimes been one member on the board—but because their voices are not extended equal political recognition and effectiveness. Where such voices would go if extended such equality, or even if they would express a single note is certainly an open question, one that the PED will encounter on more than one occasion. But for now we want to explore what it means to be an underrepresented minority in Ed City, and why that should matter.

Experiencing the Schools as an African American

Recall the expression, the Ed City Way, used to describe the loose and informal system of access that members of the school board believe is typical of the Ed City schools. If a parent cannot get satisfaction from the teacher, the principal's door is open, and if the problem is still unresolved, the superintendent or his staff is available.

The Ed City Way, though, is not how many African American parents experience the school. We heard of the unfriendly atmosphere that greeted one parent as he visited the school to monitor the education of his child during the early years of the Civil Rights movement.

In another instance, at a PED community meeting, where people were asked once again to relate their perceptions about how decisions are actually made in the school, this time focusing on discipline and suspensions, an African American mother related how only her son was suspended in a two-person fight, how in his and her mind he did not receive a fair hearing, how he was sent home on public transportation without her being informed at work, how an injured thumb went untreated, and how when she went to the district office to discuss the matter à la Ed City Way, she was asked why she was even bothering to come in since the suspension was over by that time and was told that the district could not attend to every slight injury that happened in the school.

Many things, some large some small—the failure to notify a parent of a suspension for fighting, trivializing a parent's complaint concerning due process because the punishment has already been imposed, racially differential assignments to gifted and special education classes, signs that require visitors to check in at the office, a teacher questioning a parent's presence in the school, the fact that African American but not most white children are bused around the city to designated schools, the firing of an African American teacher, the failure to retain an African American principal, the very small number of minority teacher hires— are all interpreted by African Americans as part of a history of exclusion and are largely ignored by whites who maintain that theirs is an impulse of inclusion.

Both may be right. Each event may have a reasonable explanation by itself but together these and other events over the years contribute to a sense of exclusion and feelings of alienation and with the interpretive pattern set, each new event is experienced and interpreted differently by the different groups. Thus, for example, when their calls for the hiring or retention of minority staff fail, the African American parents see another example of rejection and racism, while the school board and superintendent's office are frustrated because, as they see it, their good faith efforts seem to go unrecognized, or because "people just don't understand the budgetary constraints under which we are working."

To illustrate the difference in the way events are understood, we survey a number of racial events and encounters from desegregation in the mid-1960s to the late 1990s. We believe that these historical events and others like them serve as a benchmark for the African American community reinforcing from one generation to the next a sense that the schools do not belong to them in the way they believe that they belong to white people. Often when African Americans look at the schools, they see them as controlling and manipulating institutions. This is sad given that the decision to end segregation almost fifty years ago was taken as such a great victory. When school board members, teachers, and administrators experience this distrust in light of what they view as their own well-intended behavior, they may act in ways that reinforce it. And, because these events are largely lost to the schools' official memory, a memory that believes the Ed City Way holds equally for all, there is little opportunity to discuss the events that helped to cause it. In the end the muting of the experience of members of the African American community creates a wall of silence that both communities need to penetrate but that, often, neither can.

Desegregation, Busing, and Racial Inequities: Some Key Events

Item One: In July 1966, Ed City desegregates its ten elementary schools. There are 456 African American elementary school children in the district, and 95 percent of those children attend the virtually all–African American Rosa Parks School. Desegregation is accomplished by busing 353 African American students from the Parks School to the then nine all-white schools (thirty to forty students to each school), and busing 189 mostly white children whose parents are students at the local university into Parks School. This is called cross-busing. In the words of one school board, "No white children are being bused." He is wrong. Rather, no children of permanent white property tax paying members of the community were bused.

Item Two: In May 1968, seventy-four people, most of them African American parents, meet with school officials to describe the mistreatment to which their children have been subjected, particularly in the junior high school. Only one school board member attends—the first African American elected to the Ed City School Board.

Item Three: In June 1968, a committee of African American people concerned with education presents a proposal for change to the Ed City School Board. The board promises to consider the proposal at its July meeting. The proposal is not placed on the July agenda. The committee of African Americans walks out of the meeting.

Item Four: In January 1972, five years after the schools were desegregated, the Ed City School Board is criticized by African American parents for ignoring their contribution to the desegregation effort in a report submitted to the district office of the state superintendent of public instruction.

Item Five: In January 1976, the Ed City School District is cited by the State Board of Education for failing to comply with state desegregation regulations (*Ed City Herald,* 8 January 1976). Parks School has a minority enrollment of 51 percent, but administrators explain that a large segment of those minority children are not African American but the children of foreign graduate students. In May, Ed City learns that a special arrangement with the state has saved the school district from being cited for noncompliance with desegregation. Ed City is permitted to keep its busing plan.

Item Six: In January 1989, some Ed City parents, including a school board member, object to a redistricting and busing plan that has, as one of its goals, to balance school enrollments by socioeconomic background, just as they are racially balanced. (*Ed City Journal,* 16 January

1989) The school board member says that the administration's plan will diminish educational quality at [the top three schools] by bringing teaching down to the least common denominator. Nevertheless, socio-economic busing is adopted.

Item Seven: In March 1995, more than one hundred African American parents march on the school board, protesting the firing of two minority staff members, and calling for the hiring of more African American teachers and administrators.

Item Eight: In August 1997, the Office of Civil Rights (OCR) of the U.S. Department of Education, on the basis of a complaint made by an African American activist, finds a severe overrepresentation of African Americans in special education classifications and a severe underrepresentation in gifted programs. It obliges the district to discontinue race-based busing to achieve certain levels of minority presence in the schools located in predominantly white neighborhoods.

Item Nine: In November 1997, the same African American activist who had stimulated the OCR investigation, presents the school board with an ultimatum regarding the busing of African American children and other equity issues and threatens the board with a lawsuit if it does not comply. The board also hears from its own boundary review committee which reports on the state of busing. It decides to contract out for its own equity review.

Item Ten: In October 1998, the equity audit commissioned by the school board under the above pressure confirms the OCR's finding of underachievement by African American students in Ed City Schools.

Item Eleven: In May 1999, the school board announces that hereafter African American children living in the Rosa Parks neighborhood will attend that school.

The Impetus for Desegregation

In early July, 1963 the state legislature amended the state school code, prohibiting school boards from erecting, purchasing, or acquiring buildings for school purposes that would promote segregation based on color, race, or nationality. A fifteen-member committee, with two minority group members, was appointed in Ed City to study how this state legislation could be put into effect. Imposed segregation was not an issue for the junior high school and the high school. Those schools were desegregated because all of the children of the district attended them. Segregation was, however, a problem in the grade schools, particularly in Parks School, which was 95 percent African American.

In the 1940s and early 1950s, Parks School, which was called the Crown School before the Civil Rights movement, had a mixed student body of African American and white working-class children. But by the mid-1960s it had become overwhelmingly African American. This was due to an influx of African Americans from the South and a concomitant out-migration of white working-class people from the neighborhood. In this process, the high school performance levels of students from Parks declined to a point where some of the long-time African American residents of the neighborhood became concerned for the futures of their children. Approximately eight or nine of them constituted themselves into a Parks School Neighborhood Association. They pressed the district to come up with a desegregation plan that would bring it into conformity with the amended school code and would offer African American children residing in the neighborhood educational opportunity comparable to that being offered to white children. Although in earlier times there had been great pride in their neighborhood school, for some of the long-time residents the costs of retaining it as a neighborhood school had become much too high.

The result was that the Parks students would be bused to all-white schools, and indeed, no child was excluded from any school because of color, race, or nationality. Thus did Ed City become the first school district in the state to desegregate (*Ed City Journal*, 20 August 1966).

Initially the 1966–1967 school year produced glowing reports on the success of the integration plan. The *Ed City Journal* carried headlines such as: "Parks School PTA Pleased with Busing," and "Cross-Busing Helping Negro Children." White parents from the grade school located in the so-called "faculty ghetto" helped with the busing project. But reports began to circulate that African American children feared white children, and teachers complained that they had to work harder on lesson plans because they had classes with children at different ability levels (*Ed City Journal*, 12 March 1966). White mothers found no spaces in the Girl Scout troops for black children (12 March 1966).

Conflict in 1968

In May 1968, a month and a year famous for conflict all over the world, Ed City was experiencing its own. Two years after desegregation was instituted,

> a crowd of between 50 and 75 local residents, the majority Negro and adult, met with representatives of . . . the school district to air grievances about [the] alleged mistreatment of

Negro pupils, particularly at Ed City Junior High. (*Ed City Journal*, 16 May 1968)

The complaints of the African American parents focused on the suspensions of their children, on not being informed when their children received detention, and on reports that administrators would not allow certain African American children back into school. The district superintendent refused to discuss specific cases with the assembled parents.

The complaints from the May meeting surfaced again in midsummer. A citizens' group presented the school board with eleven resolutions regarding the treatment of African Americans in the Ed City schools. These resolutions were supposed to appear on the July agenda of the board meeting, but they did not.

Citizens representing the Parks School area charged the Ed City School Board with "unfair treatment and lack of courtesy for neglecting the list of proposals submitted by them to the board last month on the agenda of the board meeting that night." Demanding that the school board meet with the steering committee of their group, the leaders of the African American community then walked out of the meeting. The board president "retorted '[We] will not bow to the demands of any group,' explaining that the Board did not have time to meet formally on the proposals" (*Ed City Journal*, 16 July 1968).

Thus, two years into desegregation, it became clear that simply busing African American to previously white schools was not going to resolve anywhere near all of the racial issues. Indeed, African American critics said the system perpetuated de facto segregation. As the Fall 1968 school year started, the *Journal* reported more racial fights in the junior and senior high schools.

Forgetting the Contributions of the Parks School Parents

On 6 January 1972, Mr. Charles Paul, one of the leaders of the Parks School PTA, came to a public study session to set the record straight on why the African American community had supported busing—to improve the quality of education for their children and not just to mix with white folks. Addressing himself to the draft of the desegregation report submitted to the district office of the state board of education, he noted that the report failed to record the contributions of the Parks PTA to the desegregation project. The president of the school board replied that the people who wrote the report "did not know of the efforts of the Parks parents' group." But the report did take pains to praise the contributions of the all-white Community Council on Integration, and the League of Women Voters.

In correcting the report, Mr. Paul noted that the "Parks PTA wanted change for educational reasons rather than for socialization or integration." He then asked rhetorically if that goal had been filled, since Parks School children were "probably at least two years behind other pupils in the system." The director of elementary education responded that progress would be hard to determine because "so many factors were involved and tests are often culturally biased." (*Ed City Journal*, 6 January 1972)

1974: Two White Administrators Favorable to Racial Equality Leave the System

On 28 January 1974, after four years in Ed City, the white principal of the junior high resigned. He charged that the schools were returning to a repressive state, with less emphasis on the value of each individual. But he was really quitting, he said, because "of the influence which certain white middle class parents have with the Board of Education, and the Board's lack of support of administrators." He also charged that a small group of parents with an elite attitude (the PTA Council, Citizens Advisory Council, and Master Planning Committee) was "doing all the talking . . . and most of these parents are from two of the elementary school attendance areas." These parents, he suggested, "want to maintain homogeneous groupings in the schools and this makes it hard for the kids to think in terms of Black and white" (*Ed City Journal*, 24 January 1974).

A white member of the school board answered, "'White middle class' is not a cuss word" (*Ed City Journal*, 26 January 1974). This same member asked, "Who elected the first Black member to the school board? White middle class people" (8 January 1976).

A special meeting of the Ed City school board was called on 4 November 1974. The purpose of the meeting was to report on the effects of busing on the district's African American children. Ninety minutes into the meeting, the superintendent of the Ed City schools announced his retirement, effective 31 July 1975. The president of the board finally succeeded in adjourning the meeting, over the shouts and cries of the African American parents in the audience who supported the superintendent.

The sole African American member of the board read a prepared statement that said in part, "I deeply regret that more [of the superintendent's] positive ideas have not been better received by more people."

She credited him with attempting to equalize education for all students, black and white alike.

The superintendent had been under pressure from some members of the community who felt that the academic standards of the district had suffered. When asked if pressure politics had been a part of his decision to leave, the superintendent said that "the forces that are at work in this community are too complex for me to make any short comment on" (*Ed City Herald*, 5 November 1974).

Parks Parents March on the School Board, 22 March 1995

On the evening of 22 March 1995, more than one hundred people, overwhelmingly African American, marched silently from the Baptist Church to school board meeting. Each marcher carried a pink slip of paper that read, "The purpose of the march is to let the school board know that the community is not asleep AND that we care" (*Ed City Journal*, 23 March 1995). The group publicly prayed before entering the school board meeting. For more than two hours its members protested the firing of an African American principal at the high school and an African American teacher at a grade school. A leader of the group read the following statement: "We believe that it is beneficial that our children have the opportunity to learn in an environment where diversity can be . . . celebrated. Therefore it is imperative that we maintain a racially diverse staff. Retaining minority staff is and has been a problem in this district. We can no longer remain silent" (23 March 1995).

Speaking to the school board, marchers recalled past incidents of discrimination in the schools. One African American woman noted that "for more than twenty years I have been a parent in this district . . . and I have seen very little change in the way the education process is done." Another marcher, who had taken some college classes, said that when she moved to Ed City four years earlier, teachers asked her if she wanted to join the GED program. "I wanted," she said, "to feel welcomed, not stereotyped." Another woman reported overhearing one white teacher say to another about African Americans "they sit at home, watch soap operas, sit on their behinds and collect welfare" (*Ed City Journal*, 23 March 1995).

Experiences like these created an atmosphere that made it virtually impossible for many in the African American community to accept the legitimacy of the decisions of the school board. Citing policies on confidentiality in personnel matters, the board felt it could not share its grounds with the public. The marchers felt that this supported their conviction that the decision was illegitimate. In response to the demand for more minority hiring, the district's director of human resources observed that it was difficult to find qualified African American candidates for positions in the schools. For some in the community this must have been reminiscent of the summer of 1968 when the parents of these parents marched on the Ed City school board and were told by the president of the board that funds were limited for such hiring. Even though one of our informants, a white teacher who frequently disagrees with the board and has a history of supporting progressive agendas, told us that she felt that there were grounds to dismiss the principal, the reservoir of trust was too shallow to allow an uncontested decision on a matter of such symbolic importance.

1997 Verified Disparities

The woman who had served as the first African American on the Ed City school board during the early years of desegregation had subsequently received a university degree, and had been serving as a counselor at the middle school for a number of years. In 1997 she was, without warning, moved out of her office where she had access to student placement files. She had raised questions about the racial differentiations in placement, especially in math classes. The Anti-racism Caucus of the teachers' union, her church, other African American teachers, and African American parents took up her cause. There was a meeting held in which another African American teacher talked about the lack of any serious attempt to hire African American teachers at her school, of her being kept off the recruitment committee, and of inequities in special lower achieving classes at her school with only one Caucasian boy in them.

The same year, the Office of Civil Rights of the U.S. Department of Education found a strong racial imbalance of students in both special education and gifted classes. Approximately 22 percent of the children in Ed City's schools are African American. (*Boundary Review Committee Report*, 23) Yet the OCR found that 48.7 percent of the students in special education classes were African American. And only 7.4 percent of the students in gifted program were African American. The district entered into a consent agreement in which it agreed to do a variety of things, including to increase "parent and community involvement in the District's educational programs" to remedy these imbalances, and to "fully evaluate the need for any increased multicultural training and other professional development activities in order that school personnel employ effective instructional strategies with all students."

In regard to the matter of increasing parental and community participation, the district specifically committed itself to using its SBDM Committee (discussed in chapter 6) to research ways of achieving such participation (OCR Resolution Agreement, 15 August 1997, 1.)

Reviewing this history reminded us of an interview we had with an African American man who was one of the four African Americans to have ever served on the school board. When we asked him about "integration" in the schools he became very angry and said, "don't ever use that term around me. That's an insulting word, because we don't have integration. We are desegregated by law. We have problems, because the mindset of the people, too many people, is to just go along with whatever to keep the wolf off your back."

This interview took place quite early in our study and we really did not fully understand the distinction he was making until we gained an historical overview of race and education in Ed City. Indeed, there is every indication that most of the white middle-class citizens of Ed City, including those actively involved with the schools, assumed that the combination of racial desegregation and the Ed City Way had either already dealt with any conceivable racial problem or provided a ready mechanism for doing so. The Ed City Way worked for some of the people, but as an all-encompassing assurance of equity and access it has turned out to be an ideological illusion.

Busing, Power, and Racial Identities

From the very beginning busing was perceived as a serious political problem by the school board. White parents were not going to want to send their children to the school in the segregated African American neighborhood. A solution was found through the targeting of younger, temporary, non–property tax paying, and relatively powerless members of the community. These were graduate students with families living in a university housing complex called Trout Village. Because these parents were graduate students who have since left the community, they have left behind little in the way of cultural memory, but their story is an important part of the picture. It enables us to see clearly issues of race tied directly to existing structures of political and economic power, and to understand how the community at large failed then to confront many of the issues that full integration requires, issues that have been the focal point of the PED's efforts.

Desegregation began in 1966 by busing the students from Trout Village and Parks School. The grade school students from Trout Village had previously attended an all-white and relatively affluent neighborhood school, Horace Mann. The demands of the Parks parents confronted the residents of the Horace Mann district with the race issue. The desegregation plan would send African American students to their neighborhood school. The parents objected, and argued that their school was full and could accommodate no more students. The school board agreed.

But a problem remained. Where would the board find white children to send to Parks School and relieve the pressure on Horace Mann? A convenient answer was found. Trout Village, populated entirely by university graduate students and their families, was more than a mile and a half from Horace Mann. With the support of the Trout Village parents, the district was already planning to incur the cost of busing their children to Mann. So a decision was made to bus the children, but to the more distant Parks School.

Thus, Trout Village, a residential complex for transient, non–property tax paying, married students, was cut off from Horace Mann and turned into a separate district. This became the white population that was used to desegregate Parks School. While some Trout Village parents voiced angry objections, they did not have sufficient power to stop this arrangement. Since they were transient, they were also unlikely to vote in school board elections. All neighborhood schools but Parks were kept intact. No cross-busing, defined as "taking youngsters by bus from their own school and replacing them with pupils from their 'new' school," occurred. This resolution

> ruled out a fear heard from some residents—that other Horace Mann pupils, aside from those in Trout Village, would be bused away from their neighborhood school. (*Ed City Journal*, 20 August 1966)

This project ensured that no children of white, taxpaying, voting, permanent residents were bused. White children who were bused, were bused, not because of "desegregation, but [because] the pupils can culturally and educationally benefit by being transferred to other schools" (a resolution passed by the school board on 19 August 1966, *Ed City Journal*, 20 August 1966). Hence, if you were white and bused, you were bused, not because you were white, but because busing would benefit you culturally, or educationally. Busing erased race. The director of instruction for the district was clear on this, stating that in assigning "pupils from Parks to other schools, no account is taken of race. The bused pupils could include some of the minority of white youngsters too" (20 August 1966).

In his mind Ed City had no problem with racial segregation in its schools. By pure coincidence, the small minority of poor whites from the Parks District commingled with poor African Americans. Race and class meshed neatly in this instance. Ed City achieved racial balance in the schools in 1966 by cross-busing Parks students, whose places in Parks were taken by students from Trout Village. But the busing of Trout Village "pupils to Parks generally is not considered cross-busing since their previous neighborhood school, Horace Mann, ran out of room, and those pupils would have to be bused to other facilities anyway."

Thus, the students from Trout Village who were bused, were really not *bused students.* The school board argued that no additional busing is needed, "geography is in our favor . . . there never has been any consideration of cross busing to achieve integration." Of course, as one school board member noted, ignoring the children from Trout Village, "all the white children attend neighborhood schools" (*Ed City Journal,* 21 March 1967).

By the 1980s, the population of Trout Village, which had been almost all white in the 1960s, had changed. The vast majority of the residents had become foreign graduate students, most of them people of color. Thus, virtually no white people at all were being bused by the eighties. The schools in white areas were very much neighborhood schools.

However, in 1989 the district decided to bus students from lower socioeconomic, predominantly white areas to schools in more affluent neighborhoods. Thus, both race and class were accounted for in the busing system after 1989.

There has been no visible organizational activity on the part of lower income white people on the busing of their children to schools outside of their residential areas or of the treatment of their children within those schools. Perhaps, because of the muting of the class issue in American politics and society generally, poor and working-class whites have constructed nothing comparable to the web of African American organizations that serve as a collective voice in Ed City as well as in most cities in the United States with significant African American populations.

The method of one-way busing of African Americans had been discussed in the PED's community meetings since their inception. But in October 1997, an African American activist presented the board with an ultimatum. Either it sign a "Memorandum of Issues," in which it agreed to a "controlled" public school choice plan with African American parents actively participating in its design, or face litigation. In light of the findings of the Office of Civil Rights, the memorandum also demanded that the skewed placement of African American and white students in both special education and high achieving classes be stopped. Finally, it insisted that two controlled choice experts be hired, one to consult with and advise the district and one to do the same with the African American community.

The district did not sign this memorandum. It did however establish a committee to conduct an internal review of school boundaries (report submitted in December 1997). It also hired one firm, rather than the two demanded by some community activists, to perform an equity audit for the district. As indicated above, the equity auditors basically confirmed the findings of the Office of Civil Rights regarding the racially differential achievement levels in the school system. But the finding that most distressed the African Americans who listened to the auditors deliver their report in a public session was a response of educators within the system to an item on a survey conducted by the auditors. "Approximately one-half of responding educators did *not* believe that schools should be significantly changed to effectively address the needs of all students even though nearly all respondents held that schools were capable of significant improvement" (Executive Summary of the Educational Equity Audit and Climate Report).

The district appointed a committee composed of educators in the system, parents, and community people to go over the findings and recommendations of the outside auditors and recommend to the school board how it should proceed. Even before this committee had finished its work, the board, under pressure from the OCR and the threat of a lawsuit, made a decision on the busing issue. Two months before the committee reported its findings to the board, the latter declared that those African American pupils from the Parks neighborhood who were already attending schools in primarily white neighborhoods could continue to do so if their parents wished. And younger siblings who attained school age could go to the same schools. Aside from this, however, no additional pupils from the Parks neighborhood would be bused out to achieve desegregation. But the multicultural programs at Parks that were a result of sending the multinational children's population of Trout Village to Parks school would be salvaged by continuing to bus those now largely children of color to Parks.

Reading Race in Ed City

Returning to our original question: what does it mean for a minority to be underrepresented in a system where anyone who chooses to run gets on the ballot, where everyone is allowed to vote and where those who receive the majority of the votes are elected to office? One answer, specific to African Americans in Ed City, is that there is no institutional history to remind those who control education about the long train of historical events that have contributed to the way in which many African American parents interpret their children's present experience in the schools. Most people in these positions are too young to have been a part of the earlier episodes and the local history is largely forgotten even though it is played out every day through small interactions, misunderstandings, and miscommunications, through expected rebuffs and mistrust, through frustration and rejections, both imagined and real. At the community level, African Americans are remembered as a group mainly during Black History month, and on Martin Luther King's birthday, or when one of their children causes trouble. While many in the African American community have experienced an intergenerational history of exclusion, people on the school board do not have access to this history and interpret the recent Ed City experience as one of inclusion. As one school board member noted in an interview with us in 1994, "We've always had one of them (African Americans) on the school board, what's the issue?" (Interview, 28 October 1994).

It took a federal OCR investigation and a threat of a lawsuit to bring the issue to a head and to expose it in greater depth. But there are certain ironies in the story. One is how time changes how things are interpreted. Ed City was in the forefront of desegregation among mid-sized cities in the state. In the 1960s, African American parents living in the Parks district had pushed to bus their children to the other schools. At the outset, busing the largely white children from Trout Village to Park was a politically expedient way to avoid a probable confrontation with white parents who were permanent taxpaying citizens with clout. But as Trout Village became more and more populated by non-Western people of color, it opened up the possibility for the creation of an extremely progressive multicultural program at Parks that benefited all of the students there.

On the other hand, an administrator in the district who conducted a 1999 survey of parents with children bused out of Parks informs us that there is 75 percent to 80 percent satisfaction level. Under the new policy change, parents who want their children to attend any school other than Parks will have to petition as individuals. They will have to offer a reason for this special request. If the principal in the requested school determines that there is space, and accepts the reason offered in the petition, then and only then will the request be granted. Moreover, while the cost of busing was assumed by the district under the former desegregation policy, the petitioners must now be prepared to assume responsibility for transportation. This will surely be a disincentive for low income people.

So Ed City is in a new place at this point, in a trajectory that will continue to take many transmutations as the community moves through time. It has, under external compulsion but also with considerable internal chagrin over inequities revealed in its educational system, given up its desegregation policy of busing children out of Parks School area. In the 1960s, the board of education could have, but chose not to, considered a truly cross-based busing system. By 1999, busing exclusively designed to achieve racial integration had been deemed illegal by the OCR unless specifically ordered by the courts.[3] The result is that Parks area parents have gained a neighborhood school, while other schools in the district stand to lose a significant African American presence. But Parks is not exclusively a neighborhood school. It includes one of the most diverse student bodies in the nation and sustains a vital multicultural experience for its students.

Conclusion

The process of getting to this new conception of racial equity from those of the 1960s and 1970s has involved confrontation and conflict as well as negotiation and agreement. But then, how could it have been otherwise, for are American schools not a microcosm of the dynamics facing the nation at large in terms of race and class? Put in that perspective, the record of the diverse elements within this community attempting to come to grips with the education of their children has been rocky to be sure but it also has reflected an impressive level of civic discourse and activism.

Educational equity must be a cardinal principle of any democratic society. But within a multicultural society, as most societies are now, it is also one of the most difficult to achieve, as the experience of this country with desegregation, busing, neighborhood schools, social promotion, mandatory summer schooling, tracking, standardized tests, and whole child evaluations shows. There is no royal road to resolution. Even assuming good faith attempts to overcome prejudice and bias, all roads have their twists and turns, which in theoretical language we would call "contradictions," and in public policy language "unanticipated conse-

---

3. From an interview with the OCR investigator in the Ed City case (27 July 1999).

quences." It takes a strong democratic will to keep going. Ed City seems to have a strong dose of that, of which the PED is but one element.

Another, of a very different sort, is the school board itself. It is to that institution that we now turn.

The PED's Challenge to Traditional Authority: The School Board

Introduction

Different people have different ideas of what is fair or equitable, and often the same person may entertain conflicting notions of fairness. In this chapter we focus on conceptions of fairness as it is embedded in Ed City around the discourse of governance, a discourse that often takes place in relation to the school board and its practices. Our focus here brings back into consideration two of the ideas that we have explored in the preceding chapters. These are the ideas of "the Ed City Way" and "underrepresented minority." We also consider an additional idea with much currency in Ed City and elsewhere, "the best interests of children." In this chapter we examine them in relation to one another and show some of the different conceptions of democracy that lie behind them. We begin with a discussion of the school board and its authority.

Representative Authority: The School Board

In the United States, there are two mechanisms for selecting school boards, appointment and election.[1] The Ed City School Board is

---

1. L. Harmon Zeigler, et al. *Governing American Schools* (North Scituate, MA: Duxbury Press), chapter 5.

elected. This means that the board derives its authority from the electoral mandate it has received from the citizens of the district. In other words, "the People" vote for candidates who present themselves for election. As is usually the case for school board elections throughout the country, the turnout is low compared to other elections.[2] The low turnout is undoubtedly due in part to the fact that the school board elections are not held at the same time as those of the other more hotly contested elections. Since they are nonpartisan elections, the usual door-to-door party canvassing is not involved.

If citizens in the United States have lower voting rates than people in most other Western democracies for offices at the national level, by the time it gets down to nonpartisan special school board elections, turnout is typically very low, and Ed City, with a citizenry of higher than average educational level, still fits into the national pattern of low turnout with middle and higher status members of the community voting at higher rates than others. The combination of at-large and nonpartisan elections was introduced in the United States in the early part of the century (1900 to 1920) by reformers to counteract the earlier control of partisan and frequently corrupt ward bosses over urban school boards. Zeigler et al. write of the effects of these reforms that they "would eliminate the influence of party politicians . . . [and] would increase the influence of the ascendant business-professional elite and the middle classes in general and would stamp the schools with the mark of respectability."[3] Wirt and Kirst point out that this has had the effect of not only doing away with the "large working class membership" of boards but has also worked against minority membership in the larger cities.[4] While we are uncertain of working-class representation on the Ed City board historically, we do know that there was no African American representation prior to the movement toward desegregation in the mid-1960s.

---

2. The difference in voter turnout between school board elections and general, partisan elections is quite marked in Ed City. In the general election of 1996, when President Clinton was elected, voter turnout ranged between 37.18 percent and 78.34 percent among the precincts in Ed City. The total voter turnout was 55 percent. In contrast, for the school board election the following year, when four of the seven seats were up for election, voter turnout ranged between .865 percent and 35.33 percent among the Ed City precincts. Total turnout was 12.83 percent. Precincts where much of the African American population lives had voter turnouts of 11.33 percent and 8.9 percent, respectively.

3. Zeigler et al., 54.

4. Frederick Wirt and Michael W. Kirst, *Schools in Conflict* (Berkeley: McCutchan, 1977), 102.

Conceptions of Educational Democracy in Ed City

School board elections are not commonly associated with the accusative and manipulative discourse of partisan elections. Because there is a belief that educational aims should not be politically motivated, and that children should not be the subject of political wrangling, the role of the nonpartisan election is to determine who best can inhabit the space where discussions and decisions concerning the best interests of children can occur.

The view that schools and school governance are apolitical affairs has come under scrutiny in recent years. Conservatives believe that teachers' unions appeal to the apolitical nature of schools to hide their vested interest in the "public school monopoly." Progressives believe that the apolitical view hides the influence that business has exerted over the direction of schools nationally. The Right sees it as a veil for the politics of the Left; the Left sees it as a cloak for the politics of the Right. While this dualism represents common ways of thinking about educational politics in the nation as a whole, in Ed City there are three concepts through which people in the community understand the situation.

The Best Interest of Kids. In Ed City, we have heard this ideal expressed by almost all of the people on the school board and by all of the teachers in the Project for Educational Democracy (PED) in their standard refrain, "We all want what is in the best interest of kids."

The refrain reveals a certain conception of democracy and education. "The best interest of kids" speaks to the interests of children in general. It does not divide children one from another. It does not view education as a good in a field of scarcity, nor does it hold to the idea that children are engaged in a race where there will be winners and losers. Rather, it holds that education is a shared resource where the more the individual has, the richer the community life, and the richer the life of the community, the richer the life of the individual.

The Underrepresented Minority. The ideal of the best interest of children assumes that there is an objective general interest of all children that all children share (in Rousseau's terms, "a General Will") and that any well-meaning and knowledgeable person can know it. In contrast, the appeal to the needs of the underrepresented minority assumes that interests are plural and particular to the group and its members. Attempts on the part of others to speak for the group are unlikely to succeed in anything but a perpetuation of a system that serves, in the very hierarchy of the teller and the told-about, to advance the interests of the dominant group. In order to change this hierarchy the told-about must be empowered to speak for themselves. In other words, the characteristics of the children as African American or Hispanic or Asian American determines the kind of adult that can best represent their interests, that is, African American, Hispanic or Asian American adults.

The Ed City Way. Both of these ideals are at odds with the Ed City Way. The advocates of the Ed City Way believe in procedural openness as a way to mediate the difficulties that hierarchy and bureaucratic authority create. They celebrate what they believe is access of the individual across the bureaucratic divide to the source of decisions as a critical feature of democracy. Yet this conception also engenders certain concerns from the other standpoints. From the point of view of the needs of the underrepresented minority, the Ed City Way gives access largely to those whose interests are already well served by the white upper-middle-class-dominated board. From the point of view of the best interest of children ideal, the Ed City Way subverts the General Will, as Rousseau termed the objectively best law or policy for the community taken as a whole. It allows the wisest parent to speak only for her own child's education and not, as the philosopher, John Dewey wanted, for the education of all of the children in the community.

Comparison of the Conceptions of Educational Democracy

Thus, we have three different conceptions of educational democracy expressed in this single system. We have a view that conforms to an inclusive pluralist conception of democracy where a democratic society works best when different groups are represented in the decision-making body and where the will of the majority is tempered by the intensity of concern of the minority. This view holds that there are two critical features of democracy that must be present if it is to succeed. The first is that the views of all significant groups must be provided a hearing and that the intensity of feeling must be taken into account. The second is that group membership must be fluid and multifaceted so that members, if defeated on one point, will not feel defeated on all. Hopelessness is not good for democracy. Where individuals strongly and somewhat exclusively identify with one group and where the interests of that group are consistently thwarted, democracy is troubled.

We also have, in the Ed City Way, a conception of democracy that emphasizes the openness and beneficence of the individual decision makers. The hallmark of democracy is communication and the ability to keep lines of contact open in many different directions. Democracy works best when authority is reachable and changeable and when each person has access to the decision makers and understands the reasons for different policies.

And finally, we have in the best interest of children a conception that reflects Rousseau's conception of one objectively good policy for all, but departs from Rousseau's own direct participatory commitments by coming to the conclusion that this policy can be determined by elected selfless knowledgeable agents. These agents, the board members, act on behalf of the objective and discernible best interest of all the children.[5]

Each of these ideals makes different assumptions about the social good. For example, the General Will allows that there really is a social good that exists independently of any individual's desires and that it is knowable by a reasonably dispassionate observer. The interest group idea identifies the social good with the balancing of the interests of different segments of society in a way that maintains reasonable social peace, but where often "the best interest" is either not available or is not knowable beyond the expressed interests of particular parties. To say that a group is "underrepresented" is to say that many people who hold a passionate set of interests have not found sufficient outlet for their political expression and hence there is an imbalance that may threaten the social order. Here there is no objectively knowable "social good" outside of the interests and understandings of individuals and groups. From this point of view, the general will looks paternalistic at best and conspiratorial at worst—as if someone else, such as the highly educated, knew what was best for us. Those who hold a pluralistic interest group point of view might suggest instead that the highly educated segment of the population from which many members of the school board are drawn constitute a particularly powerful interest group. They would suggest that these educationally credentialed people are not necessarily any more altruistic or objective than others, but instead are in a position to best advance their own interests and those of their children.

The individualistic view embodied in the Ed City Way has a slightly different twist. It assumes that most people are basically reasonable and that most conflicts are conflicts between individuals and usually based in misunderstandings, not in fundamentally different interests. Differences are amenable to discussion and to remediation. From the individualistic point of view the General Will looks too indifferent and abstract while the interest group ideal appears too politically divisive. Of course, from those two points of view the Ed City Way is inadequate. For those

---

5. Granted we are taking some license with Rousseau because in its pure form, the General Will can only be expressed through all members of society and not through their representatives. See his *Social Contract*.

who express the best interest of children, it is a way to subvert the common good while serving a particular individual interest, while from the point of view of those who believe they are underrepresented in the social process it is a way to conceal the essentially political and dominating character of the enterprise.

Of course, the way we have stated the above presents each as if it were a pure Platonic form rather than part of the kit of mixed conceptual tools that most of us bring, perhaps only more or less consciously, to our dealings with others in our concrete life experience. To see how these "pure forms" play against one another, we now look at how people talk about the school board in Ed City.

The Ed City School Board

In describing the composition of most school boards, Frederick Wirt and Michael Kirst contend that the social characteristics of school board members have not changed much over time, at least since 1927. They report that most board members are owners of businesses, officials, managers of businesses, or professionals. Increasingly, teachers are coming on board. The board members have incomes well above the average, are conservative, and are overwhelmingly male.[6]

If one went back to 1927, or even 1950 or 1960, this description might have fit the Ed City board well. But in more recent years the Ed City board has been dominated by people with some relationship to the university, either directly or through a spouse. The skewing has been so prominent that the Ed City alternative newspaper reported that between 1981 and 1997, 80 percent of the elected board members came from the dominantly academic area, which had only 24 percent of the total population. Since the 1960s, the board has had few business people on it, has usually been more than 50 percent female, and with few exceptions has seen itself as quite liberal. From the end of the 1960s to the 1999 elections, no white working-class person without a university education has served on the board. And only three African Americans have been elected to the board, all of them since the desegregation of the 1960s discussed in the previous chapter. None of their terms of office overlapped. One African American was appointed to serve out an unexpired vacated seat but chose not to run in the subsequent election.

6. Wirt and Kirst, 104, 138.

The board is forbidden by state law to meet in secret except to discuss personnel and discipline issues. However, the fact that school board members engage in very little debate before adopting policy suggests that there is some communication about the agenda that occurs outside of the school board meetings. As one member of the school board told us:

> Board meetings really are going through reports that only the board members have seen that the audience hasn't seen, then you just sort of ratify decisions that were made outside of the meeting. The important work gets done in conversations outside—that's always the case. Because there's a lot of pressure not to have too much public disagreement and too much public debate—you want to present a united front. There's a lot of, you know, very reasonable reasons for why you don't have a lot of public debate and dissent and so, within the context of being a board member, it all makes a lot of sense that you would want all to agree and hammer out any disagreements before you come to the board meeting so that things look good. But there are a lot of problems with that. One is that the debate never really happens out in public. There's this perception that we all have the same interest at heart, which is the good of the children, but we have very different meanings for that and we just sort of assume that we all mean the same thing and we all have the same interests and so we're all representing everyone. And that's sort of naive, I think.

The board meets for both business and study sessions. While it will go out into the schools for some of its study sessions, and mix with teachers and school administrators, board members usually meet for these as well as for the business sessions in a room in which tables are arranged in a horseshoe fashion. The superintendent sits next to the president of the board, who is near the center of the horseshoe. The other six board members are arranged around the horseshoe. At the extremities of each end of the horseshoe are the assistant superintendent and other administrators in the district office. Members have a microphone in front of them and the sessions are televised on a city cable channel.

At the other end of the room, at considerable distance, is the public. At the beginning of the session, members of the public may speak to the board. There is a small table and a single microphone for that purpose. But the exchange of words, between the board and the public to the extent that there is any exchange at all, is tightly controlled at regu-

lar business meetings. The *Internal Board Operation and Bylaws* state that:
"The Board will listen but not debate with the audience." The members
listen to the public, take in what they hear, add it to what they already
know, deliberate among themselves, consult their own best internal
voice, cast their vote, and decide the matter. To the extent that there is
discussion at the horseshoe table at business meetings, much of it con-
sists of residual (i.e., not covered in administrative briefing papers prepared for the board or in study sessions) factual questions posed by
board members to administrators and the latter's responses. As the
above quote from a board member indicates, there is seldom much
debate or dissent before the public.

From the generalized point of view of a person sitting on the
board it may seem like Rousseau's process of deliberation about the
General Will at its finest. From the point of view of the powerless in the
community it may look like parents trying to model "appropriate" behavior for children whose decorum they do not quite trust.

It is our impression that virtually all of the members of the board
are committed to two things. First, they are committed to an open but
orderly school system. The openness is embodied in the ideal of the Ed
City Way; the orderliness in the tight control of public discourse at
school board meetings. Second, they are committed to what they and
others repeatedly refer to as the best interest of the children.

Virtually all of the board members take their time-consuming job
very seriously. They almost always come to the meetings. They read the
material beforehand and they come ready for making binding decisions.
Ed City's board members seem to be, in Robert Dahl's terms, outstand-
ing republican citizens who are doing their duty by fulfilling their electoral mandates.[7] They are discussing and acting in such a way that they
are fulfilling the mandate conferred upon them by the public, and they
are usually operating under severe resource constraints. These are dedicated, civic-spirited people who put in a lot of time without material or
other extrinsic political reward such as advancement toward a higher
political position, and many see themselves as representing the interests
of all children in the city, not just those whose schools are nearest to
their homes.

A former board president, Regina Green, who holds an important
administrative position outside of the school system and has herself gone
through the Ed City schools, reflects this Rousseauist understanding.

---

7. Robert A. Dahl, *Who Governs?* (New Haven: Yale University Press,
1961), 220.

Commenting on the alternative way of electing board members, the ward system, she said:

> My experience on the school board these past six or seven years has reinforced to me again and again the importance of each school board member representing the interests of each child in this district. It is extraordinarily important that school board members when they come here have a legal and moral obligation to represent all of the children of the city. I will also tell you, as an aside, that the examples of representative democracy [based on a ward system of voting] locally, statewide, and nationally, is personally an example I hope our school board never emulates. Whether conflict is healthy or not, I'm not keen on how these bodies operate. Some of these things range from embarrassing to demeaning. I think our children deserve better. But I will tell you that my primary concern is that I truly believe that every school board member should be here for every child in the city, not just the geographic area from which the school board member comes, and I think that the other form of election provides an incentive in the other direction.

Green clearly understands and subscribes to the view that there is a General Will and believes that certain kinds of political structures enhance it while others do not.

Class and the School Board

Despite Green's belief that she and the other board members act on behalf of the children of the district as a whole, not all people think or feel that their interests are represented on the board. When we interviewed Pamela Stern, the one participant in the PED whom we could clearly identify as white and working class, she raised a question about the medicating of children in the schools. She did not like the policy because she felt that it endangered confidentiality and possibly violated regulations regarding parental consent.

We asked whether she went to board meetings. She replied, "No, I do not. They make me very angry." We asked her why they made her angry. She replied: "I don't understand the decision process. Now I haven't been in years. I used to go and at that time I was so frustrated. I never quite understood the thought process."

Stern is not unusual in her disengagement. Few working-class white people seem to be engaged with the schools, and Stern's involvement with the PED, even though brief, suggests that she is more engaged than most. She sees a clear split between the school board and her community:

> I don't always feel that our school board members are in touch with our community as a whole. I come from this area and have been in this area for a long time and a lot of times our school board members don't have that much time invested in our community and may not be sticking around for a great deal of time. But the decisions they make today are going to affect us for a long time down the road. There's been instances in my dealing with the school board in the past where they had made decisions that the community, as a majority, were against. I saw that happen on several occasions in my time in the Ed City school system. I'm not sure they are always in touch with what the community is interested in or feels is best for it. I don't think that they tend to be people that have a long-term commitment within the community. You know, maybe a five or six year stint and then they're gone. Cause we do have a fairly transient community, for the university or for whatever reason. A lot of times there's not the long-term commitment.

Although Stern may not express it in these terms, she is challenging Green's attempt to speak from the standpoint of the General Will. However, she does so while embracing some of the critical features of the General Will in the abstract. In claiming that the board speaks not for the community as a whole, but only for a segment of it, namely for the professorial and administrative elite from the university, she is implicitly invoking the idea that there is indeed a community to speak for. She has rather specific ideas about where the board is not acting in line with the needs of the community as a whole, as, for example, with the medication of students.

Stern was concerned about a new policy enacted by the Ed City school administration to seek Medicaid reimbursement "for all eligible students who receive medication during the school day." As the document she presented to the PED noted, she felt that "any attempt to bring additional funds into the district is laudable"; however, the policy concerned her on the following grounds: the process used to seek the reimbursement included sending medical information about children to a private billing company, where it would be determined whether the child was eligible for Medicaid reimbursement. Stern felt that this involved a breach of the confidentiality of the children, and possibly violated regulations regarding parental consent. In addition, the document expressed concern that "there is now a financial incentive [for the district to seek to] medicate children."

Stern and the group of parents she worked with to develop the memo contacted the school district to express their concerns. She further urged other parents to call the district official in charge of this policy to express any of their concerns. By pointing out possible flaws in what might at first seem to be a logical, well-thought-out policy, Stern's actions and concerns reflect one of the critical problems with a General Will theory—the difficulty of identifying a homogeneous community whose members actually share many interests.

Stern likes to identify the real representatives of the "community" by their longevity, which she believes must represent a long-term commitment to folks like her. Yet longevity will not quite serve as an effective marker in this case. True, many of the university-related board members, unlike board President Green, have not gone through the Ed City schools themselves. However, usually their children are in the system while they are serving or have gone through it. While often having origins elsewhere, they do tend to stay in the community for long periods of their lives. The academic transients tend not to run for the school board. Moreover, longevity can be an inadequate marker for ascertaining justice and is often used to hold on to an inadequate status quo. Indeed, Stern herself gave an example of the firing of some white coaches as another example of the board's disregard of what she felt was the community's wishes. She admitted that "the murmuring was that there was some incident that one of them maybe had used a racial slur . . . I don't remember . . . It's been a long time ago . . . but those coaches had been here a long time and had a huge amount of community support."

The perception that the board does not represent her best interests, true or not, adds to Stern's alienation. When she says that she does not "understand" the decision process and the "thought process," what she means to say perhaps is that they have not worked out well for children she knows. Perhaps the fact that the decision-making process of the school board cannot be interrupted by debate from the floor adds to Stern's alienation from the process.

Recall that it was Stern in chapter 3 who, at a PED meeting, told how she tried to intervene when she felt that her daughter was being treated abusively by a teacher. She does not see the members of the board as caring about the treatment of her daughter. In her eyes, university people constitute a dominating and a oppressive group. They are both an economic upper class and the political elite insofar as control over education is concerned. She believes that in their certainty that they know best what is in the interest of the community and its children, they in fact ride over the "real" community, those who have deep roots there and will remain to face the consequences of the decisions that this elite makes. She sees this elite as nonempathetic when it comes to the interests of those outside their educational and economic circle. Stern's reaction is perhaps not surprising given the "town versus gown" rivalries that have often been manifested in U.S. communities in which there are colleges and universities.

Indeed, her perceptions and alienation from these highly educated "outsiders" are very similar to the resentment that the political theorist, Jane Mansbridge, found directed against the highly educated newcomers by the poorer and older residents of the town of "Selby," Vermont, where she studied the processes of the town meeting.[8] Like Florence Johnson, in Mansbridge's study,[9] Stern is one of the poorer members of the community and is attempting to raise children alone. Like Johnson, who believed that her children had been abused by the schools (she claimed that her son had been slapped by teachers), Stern also feels that her daughter has been abused by a teacher although intellectually rather than physically. But unlike Johnson, who felt completely powerless and never even went to Selby town meetings out of fear of humiliation, Stern at least went to some board meetings until her anger and frustration drove her away. Moreover, once the PED began to hold community meetings, she was provided with a space where she felt comfortable enough to tell her stories and listen to those of other parents, teachers, and students. In doing so she entered into a discourse that went well beyond the particular instance of what she felt was the mistreatment of her child, to a discussion of general policies about the medication of school children and the maintenance of confidentiality, and what appeared to her to be the arbitrary selectiveness of the Ed City Way. And, despite her objection to the firing of some white coaches, possibly for racial slurs,[10] she had no problem interacting with the African American participants of the PED and recognized a similarity between their situation and hers. Stern's ability to come together with different

---

8. Jane Mansbridge, *Beyond Adversary Democracy* (Chicago: University of Chicago Press, 1980).

9. Ibid., 119–121.

10. Indeed, in her interview with us she contended that there were African American parents who also supported the coaches, at the same time saying, "I'm not sure that wasn't a racial situation. I do not know. It may have come down [to that]." What she was sure about was that the school board was not discussing the issue publicly (it was a personnel issue) and that it was running against the sentiment of most of the people she knew.

sorts of people in the same community to listen to and be listened to by others was a kind of empowerment not available to Florence Johnson because no movement comparable to the PED was reaching out to her. Nevertheless, Stern remains the exception even in Ed City; she is the only clearly identifiable working-class white person who has participated in the PED.

What Interests?

Stern also presents a problem that needs to be noted for the interest group theorist. Most pluralist interest group theory begins at the point at which interests are formulated and expressed through some organized, coherent, and self-conscious articulation. The fact that Stern's is the only working-class white person's voice present at PED meetings, an informal and low-keyed group, suggests that the educational "interests" of working people such as Stern remain inchoate and underdefined. Yet a theory of political democracy that is unable to account for these inchoate "interests" and tallies only those that are already defined and organized is surely inadequate. Similarly, a theory of educational democracy that does not build into it ways to develop the skills of people who might serve to define and organize these interests is also defective. As one member of the PED put it:

> You know my father had a sixth grade education and he didn't think he was literate and would not feel very happy if he had to write a letter to a school board member and say you're not representing me on this issue. And he would probably, if he went to school board meetings, be screaming and hollering at them. You know he would have gotten very hot-tempered about it. And they wouldn't have listened. So I think we're looking for a model of communication whereby anybody can come to a school board member and can sit there on an equal basis and feel comfortable addressing them. I think there's a lot of people in this community who couldn't speak and make their ideas clear to school board members, and the school board member couldn't hear what they mean to say because they come from such different worlds.

We want to think that groups such as the PED as well as decision mechanisms such as Site-Based Decision Making (SBDM) have considerable potential in opening up and maintaining channels of communication. However, in order to fully realize such potential, it is critical that the very act of defining and organizing inchoate interests be understood as a critical part of the education of people into political democracy. In our view school boards have an important role to play in the democratic process, but where a considerable number of interests remain inchoate and underorganized school boards alone may be insufficient.

The PED has had a sense of this need and would like to find ways to service it. Participants have talked about reaching out to the people in the "trailer parks," a euphemism for the poorest of the whites despite the fact that at least some of the parks are racially mixed, but it has not been done. We suspect that lack of resources, time, and money was a factor—the PED was always a shoestring operation. Hence, we cannot say with any certainty whether many of the other poorer or working-class whites feel about the schools and their governing board the way Pamela Stern does. Nor do we know why they have not become more active in the PED, whether it is just a matter of the PED's greater attempt to reach out to the African American community, whether it is due to the absence of a class organizational network in contrast to the existence of an active African American religious and secular organizational network, whether the poorer whites are just too alienated from or intimidated by the school system, whether they lack the confidence or the time to become active, whether they just do not care, or some combination of the above. The fact that they have been absent from both the governing status quo and movements to change it does tell us that class matters, and that there are inchoate interests that have not gained any organized expression, even in the nascent form expressed by the PED.

Most interest group theories presuppose a collectivity that is available to define, express, organize around, and further a set of related interests. However, there are few such groups organized around working-class formations that concern themselves with the education of American children. It is, however, important to note that a number of the African American participants in the PED have been the most vocal in articulating the similarity of treatment and identity of interest between poor whites and most African Americans within the realm of education. Given their history it is perhaps not surprising that they are aware of the problems that arise when interests remain unexpressed and underorganized.

We can see how it matters in the perceptions that students have of each other. Despite the efforts to provide some race and class diversity in each elementary school, the kids perceive differences in the schools and their students.

As one student reported at a PED meeting, "At U school it's gritty kids; in V it's liberal academic kids; W is kids of foreign students; X is wealthy business kids; Y is trailer park poor; and Z is working class." When we asked her what "gritty" meant, she told us that it was a common term among kids, that "gritty kids are like those who congregate in the park across from the high school and smoke, chew gum, drink, sometimes do drugs, and act like they have no future."

And it matters in other terms as well. Even though there has been busing to achieve some socioeconomic as well as racial mixture in the different schools, the class balance of most schools is still shaped to a great extent by the residential pattern.

Race and the School Board

Both the General Will theories and the pluralist idea are usually presented as pure forms that work exactly as they are supposed to. Yet in Ed City this is not always the case as both the manner in which people are treated and their response to that treatment can distort the way in which issues come to the board and the force with which they are presented. The most powerful examples of this arise in the area of race relations as they have been experienced by the few African Americans who have served on the board.

The combination of nonpartisan and at-large elections, particularly the latter, has indeed diminished the role of minorities on the Ed City school board. Despite the substantial African American population, there was never any African American representation on the board prior to the desegregation of the mid-1960s.

The first African American was elected to the school board in 1968 and remained on the board until 1980. She has acknowledged publicly, without going into detail, that being the sole African American on the board was a very difficult experience. One of her supporters, who was a city councilperson at the time, went into more detail concerning the difficulties she faced and how members of the African American community would go to the meetings and defend her from the other, white board members:

They always hopped on her. We would defend her from the audience. [And, making reference to the fact that the board now has a policy whereby it refuses to debate with anyone other than another board member at its business meetings, he went on:] Well, I gotta tell you—back in those days it would've been foolhardy for them not to let us participate because that was during a period of time when tempers flared. We didn't take too much shit, to be honest, once we got involved. And had they tried to keep us from talking about various issues that were on the agenda, that would've been very difficult.

He told us that every evening before the school board meetings, he and other supporters would meet and go over the agenda items that interested them and the positions that they wanted her to take. She also enjoyed support from one of the white members of the board who had helped her in the campaign and tried to help her as a board member as well. But clearly, this was not an easy experience for this pathbreaking African American woman.

This was corroborated by another of her supporters who succeeded her on the board. This was a man who, when we asked him to characterize his predecessor's experience on the board, responded:

Pressured, problems from other board members, same that I encountered when I was on it. A lot of information was kept from the minority member of that board until the last. And I think I experienced it more. Maybe things had gotten a little bit more difficult, but I was always going to a board meeting and seeming to come in after things had started. So then I started going a half an hour or an hour early to find out what was on the agenda. I didn't know until the night of the meeting.

[Question: were they meeting without you?]

I suspect so; I have no proof—and many people, you know, when I was on the board, a lot of times I would abstain. But I had a reason for that. If I was not knowledgeable enough to vote, no way would I cast my vote. And during the firing of the principal at the middle school, I don't know why the man was fired and I was on the school board!

He suspects that there were meetings regarding the dismissal from which he was excluded and that the same thing had happened to his African American predecessor on the board.

The last African American to be elected to the school board, Robert Cleveland, who served from 1985 until 1993, was the one who so strenuously objected to our use of the word *integration*. He told us that "racist attitudes and behavior" exist on the school board itself, as well as in the school. He went on: "They [the other school board members] 'looked' at me. At least I thought so. Anything I had to say was voted down. I told them about it!"

Cleveland continued to occupy his seat but as a form of protest remained silent during board deliberations after the board sustained a list of suspensions that included his own daughter. The first time he heard of the PED was when we interviewed him. He subsequently became a participant in it.

The issue of the "look" is very interesting. It came up again when Edith Jones, an African American woman who was active in the PED for a while and subsequently ran unsuccessfully for the board, described her feelings when she spoke to the all-white board during the protest over the firing of the African American principal and teacher:

> The part about them being all white didn't really bother me. What bothered me was how they looked at me or looked at the audience. You know, it's sorta like . . . I don't know if you've ever seen this before, but do you know how to look blank? and placid? where people don't even know what you're thinking? To see this board exercising its power, you know, I thought to myself: "This doesn't feel right, you know? My inferiority may be something that's imaginary. And maybe your [the board members'] superiority, in my perception, is something that I've imagined too. But the point is, the reality is, that you [the board] do have to work with people like myself who, perhaps because of the systems and the powers that have been in place for many years, you know what I mean? . . . if there's a problem in the school, will you handle my child, will you deal with my child the same way you would deal with a child from a middle-class neighborhood? Will you treat my child the same? Do you really love my children? I feel intimidated by you. I should feel you welcome the input of everybody."

What is perhaps surprising is that African Americans, three of them between 1993 and 1998, have continued to present themselves but have been defeated. This disturbs the white board members. In the 1997 elections, an African American candidate presented himself rather late in the game. A white board member said to one of us that she and some of the other board members up for reelection discussed the desirability of one of them withdrawing in support of the African American candidate. But, she asked rhetorically, which one would do it? None did.

We had the following exchange with George Frank, the liberal board member mentioned in chapter 2 who tore up the corporate proposal of the Fortune 500 corporation in front of the then superintendent, Jimmy Fox.

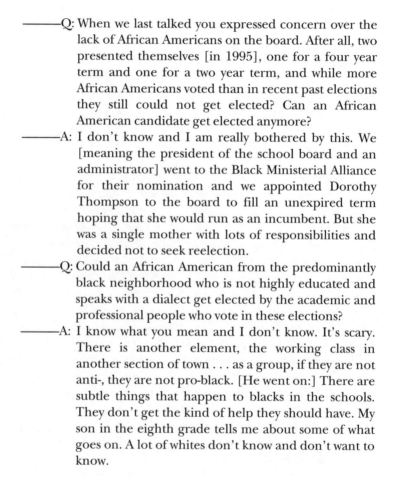

———Q: When we last talked you expressed concern over the lack of African Americans on the board. After all, two presented themselves [in 1995], one for a four year term and one for a two year term, and while more African Americans voted than in recent past elections they still could not get elected? Can an African American candidate get elected anymore?

———A: I don't know and I am really bothered by this. We [meaning the president of the school board and an administrator] went to the Black Ministerial Alliance for their nomination and we appointed Dorothy Thompson to the board to fill an unexpired term hoping that she would run as an incumbent. But she was a single mother with lots of responsibilities and decided not to seek reelection.

———Q: Could an African American from the predominantly black neighborhood who is not highly educated and speaks with a dialect get elected by the academic and professional people who vote in these elections?

———A: I know what you mean and I don't know. It's scary. There is another element, the working class in another section of town . . . as a group, if they are not anti-, they are not pro-black. [He went on:] There are subtle things that happen to blacks in the schools. They don't get the kind of help they should have. My son in the eighth grade tells me about some of what goes on. A lot of whites don't know and don't want to know.

But even the most conservative member of the board, the one who told us that he tried to represent business interests, finds the racial exclusion difficult to take:

Until four years ago we did have, and had for quite some time, at least one. I'm deeply disappointed that we don't have any now . . . It, in a way, gives us problems because decisions that are not made with any sense of race can be cast that way because there was not a minority participating in the decision. We probably have become more sensitive to the issue when there is not a minority because we have all tried very, very hard from a white perspective to not step on their toes. But we're not succeeding and that sometimes really irritates me.

But it takes considerable courage for an African American, especially one who has no connection with the university and backing from elements within the academic community, to run for the school board. We heard how daunting the prospect of such a candidacy was from an African American woman at a PED community meeting on 7 March 1996. This was the only PED meeting that the superintendent of schools attended and he was making the point that there needed to be more diversity on the board. The African American woman responded:

> Maybe it's too intimidating. Someone approached me to run, but then all of the things that I would have to deal with. I felt intimidated. It would have to start with the parents getting lots of years of good schooling themselves. With me, there's not a lot of me out there. I'm black and everything else. I think that it's the fear, not knowing [here she is talking about her own fear of being thrust in over her head]. They'll *look at* me and say "another ignorant parent."[11]

Here we have the fear of being *looked at* again in the way that Robert Cleveland had felt *looked at* by his fellow board members, that Edith Jones felt *looked at* when she spoke before the all-white board. In the perception of African American people who try to make a difference, or who even contemplate trying to make a difference in this community that sees itself as being very liberal and tolerant of diversity, the very way that African Americans feel *looked at* tries this comfortable majority self-image and reflects back to the minority a very different story of what the board's educational policy making is all about.

Indeed, the use of the words *look* and *looked at* reminds us of the use of the concept of "the look" and "looking" *(le regard, regardant)* by Jean-Paul Sartre in *Being and Nothingness,* where Sartre writes:

---

11. This community meeting was the only one attended by the superintendent. When this woman asked if it would not be possible for an inexperienced person going onto the board for the first time to concentrate on perhaps one issue for a while, the superintendent offered to work with her. He was attacked by another African American woman for being "condescending."

The "we" in "we are looking at them" can not be on the same ontological plane as the "us" in "They are looking at us." There is no question here of subjectivities qua subjectivities. In the sentence, "They are looking at me," I want to indicate that I experience myself as an object for others, as an alienated Me, as a transcendence transcended."[12]

Although Sartre uses the concept of "the look" ontologically, arguing that the look is an essential component of all human beings and their interactions with others, we see it as a good heuristic device for attaining a better understanding of the way material and status differentials constructed specifically around race inhibit communication and dialogue about educational practices that might be reproducing that very racism. Those we interviewed felt like alienated "me-others." They did not feel that they were extended the requisite social recognition to be part of the "We-community" constituted by the largely middle-class, highly educated whites who were in control of the schools. Yet these schools would play a large role in determining the futures of their children.

The PED's attempt to "break the ice" was intended to be the initial step in construction of a "We-community" based upon reciprocal regard and recognition, which they hoped would ultimately be given concrete manifestation by inclusion in the decision-making processes.

The View from Within

We do not want to simplify or overstate the situation. Although racially homogeneous since 1993 and sharing similar class and cultural/social characteristics, there are sometimes widely different understandings among the board members. For example, the reaction of the board president to the meeting at which African Americans marched on the board, the meeting so passionately described by Edith Jones as one of blank stares, was described by the president of the board to us in very positive terms:

> What you have is meetings where people who had a complaint or a grievance or a disagreement felt comfortable enough to come and express it in public. . . . At the meeting where the African American community came out I would say that there

---

12. Jean-Paul Sartre, *Being and Nothingness,* trans. Hazel Barnes (New York: Philosophical Library, 1956), 414–415.

was only one or maybe two personally acrimonious and angry
nasty exchanges . . . and I will tell you that each and every one of
the black pastors who was at that meeting came up to me personally afterwards and said, "Thank you very much for welcom-
ing us here. Thank you very much for the way you ran this
meeting. Thank you for hearing us out. We're very interested
in continuing this dialogue with you." Now, I can't tell you what
they said when they went away. I can only tell you what they said
to me that day.

Yet when we raised the issue of the African American firings
(again, the teacher was reinstated) and that very board meeting with
another board member, the immediate response was tears and we had to
pause in the interview so that this member could regain composure. She
then told us: "That's the only night as a school board member that I have
ever truly lost sleep."

There have also been differences among the members of the
board on the more general question of procedures and the refusal to
engage in dialogue with the public. As one might imagine, this tends to
correlate with their attitudes toward the PED, which stands for a participatory dialogic process. The longest-serving member of the board was a
regular at the PED's community meetings. Then in 1996, Sara Holmes, a
graduate student at the university who was an active participant in the
PED successfully ran for the board. Two other board members attended
at least one PED community meeting.

One of the latter, George Frank, the early advocate of SBDM and
of the democratization of education, was the most conflicted. He said in
an interview:

I know that some don't think that we are open. But what could we
have done to be open? I know that my own rhetoric is being
pushed back in my face and I am troubled by that. But we decided
that we won't engage in argument. We try to listen politely. To do
otherwise has the potential to become a shouting match. We don't
intend to blow them off.

I know that there are two sides to this and I believe in them
both.

The General Will Theory Rebuffed: A Change
in the Representational Mechanism

William Purcell, the kindergarten teacher who at the initial community meetings of the PED had unsuccessfully argued that the group

should exclude administrators and board members from its meetings until it built a more solid communal relationship between teachers, parents, students, and community members, disappeared from PED activities immediately after his view was rejected. But he reemerged in 1998 to initiate a different effort. This was to change the method of election of board members to a ward system. This white teacher believed that this system would offer a greater probability of African Americans gaining seats on the board than did the at-large system. This was also the conventional political science wisdom.

After attracting a number of both white and African American people to his cause, he and several others approached the school board, which had recently been elected, and formally asked them to initiate a referendum to change the method of election. The board was overwhelmingly against such a change and it was in this context that board member Regina Green made the statement that we quoted above that each member must represent the best interests of all of the children in the district. Rebuffed by the board, the only other option available to Purcell and his citizen group was to begin a petition process in the community to get the issue on the ballot as a referendum item in the coming elections. This was a major undertaking, and he came to a PED meeting to ask for help. This presented the PED with a dilemma. While they agreed with the proposition that a ward system would increase the probability of African American representation, the timing was off given their own strategy and it was far from certain that the requisite number of signatures would be gathered in the short time left to get on the ballot. In the minds of the PED members, their own effort was devoted to trying to devolve power from the board and to make more inclusive the decision-making process within the individual schools, neither of which would be facilitated if the board reverted to seeing the PED as a confrontational antagonist. And the hostility among board members to the ward system and to new elections so shortly after the last one was obvious. Thus, the PED gave no public support to the referendum drive. But the teachers' union leadership offered William Purcell's group the same meeting space that it had made available to the PED. And some active in the PED would often show up for the meetings and lend their personal support to the effort without engaging the PED itself.

The requisite number of petition signatures was obtained and the referendum passed in 1998. Both the efforts of Purcell's group and the fact that there were other electoral contests on the ballot led to a substantial voter turnout, certainly more than is usual for school board elections. The voters favored the change. The areas of the city that came out most strongly for the change were the two most heavily African

American voting districts, coming in with a combined 79.5 percent "yes" vote. Next came the white or mixed-race working-class districts with 68.5 percent "yes" vote. The more academic and more affluent wards came in with a lower 51.2 percent "yes" vote. In only two voting districts was there a "no" vote and they were by slim 53–47 percent and 51–49 percent margins. The assumption that people in Ed City by and large understood and accepted the combined good effects of the General Will and Ed City Way suffered a severe blow.

Although a new board election would have to take place, the sitting board still had the power to draw up the districting map. The African American activist who was responsible for the Office of Civil Rights investigation of the district and who had threatened to take it to court, presented a map that he felt would maximize the chance of African American representation on the board. Two other maps were proposed by sitting board members. One of those was selected.

In the actual elections, held in the spring of 1999, no African American board members were elected despite the fact that three ran. Two candidates were disqualified because their ballot petitions were improperly filled out and they had signatures on them of people who were not registered to vote. Ironically, the third ran against Sara Holmes, the one incumbent board member who was also a PED activist and involved in the change process that will be discussed in the next chapter. Holmes prevailed. Once again there was agonizing on the part of a sitting board member over whether to withdraw, leaving the African American candidate without opposition and the voters without a choice, which is not all that unusual in school board elections. Holmes decided not to withdraw, and her remaining on the board would prove to be of crucial importance in terms of the alignment of positions taken by the Equity Committee, discussed in the preceding chapter, and by the District Committee, to be discussed in the next chapter.

CHAPTER SIX

The Meeting of Bureaucratic and Dialogical Authority: The District Committee

Introduction

The school board in Ed City has a clear and traditional basis of authority. The decision-making power of the board is rooted in the electoral mandate enjoyed by the board members. They publicly declare their candidacies and they appear on a ballot during an election held at a different time from the partisan elections. Those who get the most votes for the number of seats up for election are declared the winners. Aside from their nonpartisanship, these elections follow the conventional norm of our political system. That is to say that those who present themselves as candidates in elections and get more votes than their competition have authority vested in them to make legitimate decisions for the community. This is usually referred to as representational authority. Authority is derived through an election in which those with the most votes are granted legitimacy to interpret and define the collective interests of the voters and to transform them into the action framework of binding policy.

However, there is much more to the picture than this. For example, the school board is involved with another kind of authority when it bargains with the teacher and support staff unions: contractual authority. Here the board cannot simply make deliberative decisions on its own. It has to bargain, to strike the best deal that it can with the unions. The contract itself is a kind of authority that both the board and the unions can invoke if either feels that there has been an infringement of the negotiated agreements. In addition, there is the professional authority of teachers that is derived from presumptions about their understanding of a specialized body of knowledge and the need to extend the child's identity beyond the boundaries of the parent. There is as well the authority of the parent, an authority that is derived from presumptions about the interests of individual children and about the benefits for the child when a parent or other closely related adult is available to represent that interest to the community at large.

In a large public school system representative and contractual authority are executed through a bureaucracy and its authority is exercised within the context of a rule-based system, a clear chain of command and a precise system of evaluation and accountability. Of course, as many have pointed out, bureaucrats are also people and have concerns and interests of their own that can be separated from those of the community as a whole. While contractual authority typically is based upon acknowledged partiality and self-interest, representational and bureaucratic authority appeal to the "public good."

Perhaps the most interesting characteristic of the Project for Educational Democracy (PED) is how it has opened up the issue of authority and called into question the idea of the "public good" that representational and bureaucratic authority often appeal to. Instead, it wants to supplement this idea with what the regional director of the union calls the "real folk" to highlight the authority of underrepresented parents and the need for greater participation on the part of their communities. The PED saw the empowerment of the underrepresented minorities as necessarily entailing a devolution of authority from the school board to the individual schools. Some contemporary theorists of greater citizen participation[1] would see this as filling a gap that exists between distancing and excluding representative state institutions that operate under an abstraction called "the public good," and the union director's conception of the "real folk."

Just as the idea of "the public good" is expressed through bureaucratic authority, the idea of the "real folk" can be expressed in terms of wider participation and dialogical authority. Rather than a generalized rule-based system with a clear chain of command and system of account-

---

1. For example: Benjamin Barber, *Strong Democracy* (Berkeley: University of California Press, 1984); Seyla Benhabib, "Toward a Deliberative Model of Democratic Legitimacy" in Benhabib, ed. *Democracy and Difference* (Princeton: Princeton University Press, 1996), 67–94; John Dryzek, *Discursive Democracy* (Cambridge: Cambridge University Press, 1990); and Paul Hirst, *Associative Democracy* (Amherst: University of Massachusetts Press, 1994).

ability, the ideal of dialogical authority assumes an open-ended system in which rules, the division of labor, and systems of accountability are objects to be determined by deliberation among the relevant parties.

The idea of the public good is deeply rooted in Western political thinking, from Plato's idea of justice and Aristotle's idea of citizenship through Rousseau's postulation of a General Will to which we referred in the preceding chapter. It highlights the distinction between private and public and the need to evaluate policy in terms of an overriding general interest. The classical Platonic and Aristotelian view, unlike Rousseau's, does not emphasize the need to widen participation in determining the character of that good.

In contrast, the union director's idea of real folk emphasizes the need to involve the participation of a wide number of people from different backgrounds in the determination of policy. The difference is that the classical conception allows that the common interest may be entrusted to those with "superior knowledge." Today this is usually interpreted in terms of technological or scientific expertise, or a certain level of education, whereas as an advocate of the real folk the union director is skeptical of any claim to legitimacy based on these criteria alone. Because the public good connects to a certain end (e.g., to assure that students develop the skills and civic commitment appropriate to the modern nation state, society, and economy), the idea places less emphasis on the means or process of decision making and more on the quality of the decisions that are made.[2]

The idea of the real folk or the real people, indicating a certain understanding of the "democratic citizen," is rooted in another part of democratic theory, that is, that part that emphasizes the importance of direct participation. It is expressed, at least ideally, in those American institutions so admired by Tocqueville, the all-inclusive New England town meeting and the jury system where selection as a juror carries with it no formal educational requirements, but where duties entail dialogue and deliberation.[3] Whereas the idea of the public good directs attention to the quality of the decisions that are made and asks whether they are good for the society as a whole, the concern for the "real people" is about the scope of participation and whether decisions are being made by a sufficiently broad segment of society.

---

2. Eamonn Callan, *Creating Citizens: Political Education in Liberal Democracy* (Oxford: Oxford University Press, 1998).

3. For a discussion of the relationship between the ideal of inclusivity and the actual practice of the town meeting see Mansbridge, *Beyond Adversary Democracy*, 39–135.

Of course, in actual deliberations things are never this clear cut. Those who are concerned about the real people and who want to increase the scope of participation will find ways to assure others that it is not merely a quantitative issue, but that the broadening of participation is critical for the quality of the decisions as well. And those who focus on the quality of decisions must also find ways to argue that the decisions made represent the real will of the community as a whole.

In this chapter, we will focus on the dynamics that occur as those who are most concerned with the abstraction called the public good, especially members of the school administration, finally meet those who are concerned with the abstraction called the real people, especially members of the PED. The setting for this meeting is a group formally called The District Site Based Decision Making (SBDM) Committee or, more simply, the district committee. The core group consisted of one parent, two school board members (one of whom lost his seat during the process but remained as an additional parent/community member), three teachers of whom two were also parents, and three administrators including the superintendent.[4] Two of the teachers, Marcy Bright and Rhonda Silver, and one member of the school board, Sara Holmes, were also active participants in the PED. The committee was convened on schedule by the superintendent two years after the letter of agreement between the union and the board, which agreed to examine the issue of SBDM. Its first meeting was in early Fall 1996.

The Teachers' Union and the Creation of the District Committee

Before we examine the dynamics of the district committee and the issues that arise when the ideal of the public good comes into conflict with that of the real people, it is useful to return to the role of the union in maintaining the concern with SBDM, and the shift that this entails in some conventional ways of thinking about the role of unions in education. Recall that the district committee came into being not by a decision of the board of education as a deliberative and policy-making body, but by its encounter with the teachers' union in the process of bargaining in

---

4. Although somewhat more stable in membership than the PED community meetings, attendance was rather fluid and some members stopped participating for personal reasons. This was the case with one noncertified staff member and three student participants. Other parents and community members came on occasion.

order to arrive at a contract. Both the national and the local contexts are important for understanding how this committee came about.

A union is often thought of as just a traditional interest group. Indeed, historically the major focus of the teachers' unions has been on salaries, benefits, and working conditions, that is, engaging in typical self-interested and adversarial bargaining in the same way that such bargaining manifests itself in the private sector. In the 1990s, the attacks on public education were often accompanied by attacks specifically on the teachers' unions for having a narrow vision and for protecting teachers who were not meeting the needs of children in the public schools.

Many Republican politicians, some market-oriented economists, some business leaders, and members of certain religious groups have advanced the idea of vouchers that would provide parents with public support to send their children to private schools, a sector of education which typically pays very low wages and is extremely difficult to unionize. While the groups mentioned above have rarely been particularly friendly to unions, the voucher idea was also gaining appeal among some members of minority communities. Although the relationship between the unions and members of these communities has historically been a mixed one, most minority people of color belong to income and occupational categories that the unions cannot afford to alienate.[5] Yet many will argue that it is precisely children from these minority communities that the schools have failed the most. Given the weakened position of public education as well as the weakened position of unions nationally, there is an understanding among many of the more enlightened union members that they must not repeat the mistakes of the past, when workers and minorities were pitted against one another in a struggle for jobs. They have no interest in repeating the notorious experience of Ocean Hill-Brownsville in New York in the late sixties where the union found itself pitted against the African American community.

Thus, when the union moved to advance the cause of SBDM it was not simply because of an enlightened director who had an interest in extending democratic decision making, although this was certainly a part of the picture. It was also because the union needed to advance its own cause by solidifying support for public education from one of its more natural constituencies.

---

5. For an interesting discussion of the political attack on the teachers' unions, see Peter Applebome, "GOP Efforts Put Teachers' Unions on the Defensive: Reform Issues at Stake," *New York Times*, 4 September 1995, 1:7.

A Complex Webbing of Authority

We mentioned in an earlier chapter that the PED, as an advocacy group for more inclusive decision making, required an engine to advance its ideas. For a considerable amount of time it was unclear where this engine would come from.

If we review some of the early debates within the group and analyze some of its early activities such as the community meetings and the M&M episode, there is clearly a romantic strain present. The engine would arise from the community itself, with the PED serving as but a facilitator for clarifying and effecting what the community already wanted. Sometimes, as with the "reclaim ownership of our children's education" flyer, this romanticism bordered on an insurgent activism. The community would march on the school board, as it had done to protest the budget cuts and the firings, and "reclaim" its schools, with perhaps a little help from the PED. Yet given that most members of the PED were employees of the board, given that some critical members of the African American community were not thrilled by the PED's vision, given that most of the PED members were not easily given to such activism and that they didn't see the board as a homogeneous group of enemies, and given that the support of other teachers was uncertain at best, the insurgent model was never pursued wholeheartedly.

Perhaps the turning point came at one of the early community meetings where William Purcell, the kindergarten teacher who would leave the PED and come back to initiate the movement to change the way of electing school board members, with the union director's support argued vehemently against inviting board members to become a part of the PED. At this meeting, all but one of the other teachers, Rhonda Silver, felt that this went against the very idea of inclusive decision making. Thus, although at the time no active board members answered the general invitation sent to them and the community, it was clear that change would not occur through direct political confrontation.

With that avenue closed, the PED needed to find other ways to advance its idea. One way, the most obvious, was to return to the wording of the letter of understanding between the union and the board and to use the contractual obligation that the letter of understanding created to initiate the move toward SBDM.

Of course, the letter of understanding left a lot of room for interpretation. An obligation to summarize or to develop a philosophy does not read like an obligation to implement, although from the beginning the union director read it as such. And, more importantly, the term *SBDM* can be read in many ways, some of which need not entail the inclusivity that the PED was seeking. As the superintendent participated in the formation of the district committee, it became more and more likely that summarizing would entail implementing, but some of the fundamental tensions were also to appear. The most critical of these tensions was the potential gap that can occur between participation and inclusiveness. It is quite possible to increase the level of parental involvement in decision making without also increasing the kinds of parents who are involved in making these decisions.

Once the first meeting of the district committee was called by Joe Williams, the superintendent, these issues began to surface. And, as they did, the district committee became a place in which the different forms of authority, which we mentioned above, began to engage one another as if performing a sometimes subtle and sometimes not so subtle dance. Indeed, even the birth of the committee itself was clouded by a sometimes useful but sometimes dysfunctional ambiguity about the source of the committee's authority. The ambiguity is highlighted by the role of the superintendent in constituting the committee.

The superintendent called the first meeting of the district committee, but in deference to the idea of participation and inclusiveness he did not identify the members of the committee. With the exception of the appointment of two administrators, the seats on the committee (if we can speak in such definite and formal terms when the only factor limiting the size of the committee was the size of the room in which the meetings were held, people's awareness of the meeting, and the desire of people to serve) were filled as a result of people responding to a prominently placed newspaper article in which people were invited to join and were given the contact phone number. In addition, flyers were distributed at elementary schools during registration and the union announced the committee's formation in its newsletter and urged teachers to join. Of course, PED members were also busy trying to recruit members. There was a special effort made to get African American participants and two of the early African American members came from the PED, and both the administrators and teachers on the committee made strong, but only partially successful, efforts to recruit others.

The only exception to this selection procedure was the appointment of the administrators on the committee. The superintendent notes, quite accurately, that the two additional administrators (besides himself) on the committee, had both volunteered. Yet when he called for "volunteers" it was at a meeting of principals and assistant principals where his bureaucratic authority was quite evident. The two volunteers were Elgie Clucas, a white elementary school principal who had had experience with SBDM in another district, and Sidney Smith, an African

American assistant principal in the middle school who subsequently proved to be antagonistic to the idea.

The authoritative ambiguity was also expressed by the relation of the district committee and its members to the school board. Ultimately, of course, whatever the district committee came up with would have to be accepted by the school board, as the body that holds representative authority in the community. However, to just focus on this makes the deliberations appear more formal than they were and neglects the interesting way in which different forms of authority interacted within the space that the district committee provided.

Given Joe Williams's support and the fact that the board had a contractual obligation to examine SBDM, the committee might appear to be simply another arm of the state, and the PED might seem to have acquiesced to the requirements of the state in order to attach its idea to an effective engine. Yet the randomness of the committee, the rather haphazard way in which some of the members were "appointed," the ambiguous position of the superintendent and the board members who sat on the committee indicates that it was both more and less than an instrument of representative and/or bureaucratic authority. It had its own character existing somewhere between state representative and bureaucratic authority on the one hand, and extra-state dialogical authority, that is, the authority that is evaluated in terms of an equal exchange among equal participants, on the other.

What we see here is thus a political arena with vague boundaries, situated somewhere in the interstices between the state (legally elected school board and its formal administrative arm) and civil society (unions, PED). The authority relationships are complex and people are taking risks by encountering each other in such an uncertain space. The superintendent, his subordinate administrators, the tenured and untenured teachers, school board members who are stepping outside their official role, parents who have traditionally assumed a more deferential PTA role, and students who respond to the coaxing of their teacher all come to the table to discourse with one another supposedly freely as equals. Aside from the risks entailed in the very process of the committee deliberation, for example, teachers offending administrators with authority over them or parents and students offending teachers, there are the outcome risks. Will the school board be willing to delegate its power? Will administrators be stripped of some of their power but still be held fully accountable by the board and any new school councils or committees? How much teacher autonomy is at risk? Will the union be able to protect tenure? To whom will parents be able to appeal decisions made under any new system? Will accountability be sufficiently assured?

Will decisions advance educational quality? Will students be able to exercise an informed and uncoerced voice? Will the new system really open the door to the excluded or will people of the same race and class who presently dominate the system wind up dominant in the new one with even less recourse to appeal and remedy since administrators and the board will lose some of their authority to redress?

The District Committee in Operation

With this background, let's return to the tension between the public good model of education and its real people counterpart and examine it in the context of the interpersonal dynamics that take place within the committee's deliberations. We take the real people as an ideal type to be favored by advocates of dialogical authority in which positions shift from participant to participant relatively independent of role. In contrast, we take the public good to be an ideal type favored by advocates of bureaucratic/representative forms of authority in which the hierarchy of functional roles guides the discursive form. When some people are (or are perceived as) operating under norms of authority associated with one ideal and others are (or are perceived as) operating under the norm of authority associated with the other ideal, agreement will be complicated and conflict is likely to occur.[6]

The implicit but operational norms of the PED members on the committee were dialogue and consensus. Others were more attached to bureaucratic/legal norms and were there because they occupied a certain position in the bureaucracy. As a result of that position, they were expected to address the issue of SBDM that had been expressed as an attachment to the contract that had concluded the strike. In other words, they were there within the context of their position in the rule-based bureaucracy and were accountable to its expectations and evaluation procedures.

---

6. This is a variant of Jane Mansbridge's point that the assumptions behind two ideal forms of democracy, "unitary" and "adversary," are very different. But it also calls into question the ease with which her prescription that groups must be prepared to switch from one mode to another depending on the configuration of interests involved can indeed be executed. Such a switch might be useful in particular contexts. But those who initially try to initiate shifts from one mode to another can just as easily be viewed as duplicitous and in violation of the basic rules of the game. See Mansbridge, especially Part IV.

Superintendent Williams called the first meeting, which was held in the conference room of the administration building. This space was familiar to the principals because it was where the superintendent held administrative meetings. It was a place that signaled the presence of bureaucratic authority, a signal that was amplified as the participants took their places. From the very first meeting the superintendent sat at the head of the table occupying the same place that he holds when he chairs official meetings. During the course of the district committee meetings, he would be flanked by the two administrators and the other participants would occupy the remaining seats.

He initiated the discussion at the first meeting by saying that he had looked into the situation in all of the schools and that his "initial reaction regarding the autonomy of the schools was very positive. There is lots of decentralized stuff. A good number of schools are doing site-based." He went on to mention that there were "unique district-wide things that were also going on," and he cited a school calendar committee, the superintendent search committee that interviewed and ultimately selected him, a task force committee on expenditure reduction, program councils, the PTA, and discipline committees. All of these activities involved a wider group of participants and were used as examples to show how the district involved various kinds of individuals in its activities.

Williams's statement and the examples that followed it displayed two different sides of SBDM, which, while remaining undifferentiated, served to confuse the deliberations. The first of these involved the discretion allowed individual schools in determining their own agenda, a discretion that might or might not involve parents and other community members. This might be thought of as the *decentralized component* of SBDM. The second involved activities that existed on a district-wide level and which did involve parents and people from the community. This might be thought of as the *participatory component* of SBDM.[7]

---

7. In fact, one of the first tasks that the district committee set for itself was to draw up a questionnaire to determine how principals, teachers, parents, and students viewed decision making in their schools in the four areas of curriculum and instruction, personnel, budget, and building policy. The response of the principals was particularly interesting because it showed a wide variety of patterns of decision making, from the principal making the basic decisions him or herself, to teachers making them with the principal giving up the option of a veto, to parents and community people having a role on committees that were only advisory to the principals or the teachers. While this variety itself could be seen as evidence of the leeway at the sites and thus SBDM, it obviously fell short of what the PED was aiming at.

Although these different components of SBDM remained tangled, Williams was clearly affirming one of the features of bureaucratic authority—the right to define terms operationally in light of the situation and issues at hand. In contrast, one of the features of dialogical deliberation is that it provides occasions to penetrate and challenge official definitions when the circumstances or the situation seem appropriate from a certain standpoint. For example, as Williams continued to hold that the district had considerable levels of SBDM already in practice, the school board was entering into the agreement with the Office of Civil Rights of the U.S. Department of Education (OCR). In the context of this investigation, the superintendent's office had "asked," in conformity with the agreement it struck with the OCR, "the [District] Site Based Decision Making Committee to examine the research on ways to increase . . . parental participation." The district was to demonstrate compliance with this by mid-winter, 1998. Thus, at the very least, the district had agreed in the context of the civil rights hearing that African Americans constituted an underrepresented minority, and on more than just the school board where it was completely unrepresented. Nevertheless, the superintendent and other members of the committee continued to contest how much SBDM the district already had.

Thus, three different definitions of SBDM were floating around at the beginning of these meetings.

1. SBDM as local control;

2. SBDM as parent/community participation in the governance of individual schools;

3. SBDM as the involvement of underrepresented minorities in the governance of schools.

A lot of the static on the committee resulted from the superintendent asserting one of these definitions as the guiding one for the committee, while the PED members had placed their highest priority on another one. In other words within the context of the district committee meetings, the superintendent understood and spoke about SBDM as primarily and operationally concerned with increasing the scope of decisions allowed to individual schools. The participation of parents was also an issue, although his examples suggest that he felt that the district had already gone a long way in meeting this need. He also knew that the district had a problem with minority representation, and felt that the district committee would be a useful place in which to address this problem. However, at that time it was not clear that he saw this as an inherent element of SBDM.

For members of the PED these priorities were reversed. Their most important concern was to increase the role of underrepresented minorities in the governance of schools, and then, perhaps, in the other bodies that the district might establish. Increasing the scope of decision making at the level of the individual school, was of concern only if enhanced minority participation went along with it. This difference accounts for a considerable amount of the friction between some members of the committee, and involved the superintendent in a rather constant open conflict with Rhonda Silver, one of the two teacher-PED members on the committee. The superintendent would say, "We already have it" or, "We already have considerable SBDM," and Silver would counter, "We do not." This is why the more empowering second letter of understanding, proposed by the union and contractually accepted by the board of education one year after the district committee had been functioning, substituted the expression "shared decision making" for SBDM.[8]

Another source of friction was the ambiguity between the bureaucratic authority represented by the superintendent and the other two administrators on the committee and the dialogical authority preferred by PED members. For example, Sidney Smith, the African American assistant principal largely followed the superintendent's line, but went somewhat further because he voiced serious concerns and reservations about the very idea of SBDM. He contended that SBDM was a violation of the state's school code, which made the boards of education responsible for decisions in the schools. He claimed that the school board could not delegate such powers to school councils of parents and citizens and that if the inclusive decision-making bodies in the schools messed up, the blame would still unfairly be placed on principals and administrators. They would be left holding the bag. Moreover, he equated SBDM with the power to hire and fire principals and he argued that where this had been done by school councils in areas about which he had knowledge it had turned into "hatchet jobs."

---

8. While the first letter of understanding just mandated the committee to "summarize the practice and procedures of site based decision making across the district and develop [sic] philosophy that reflects our mission and strategic plan," the second letter of understanding charges the committee "to develop a consensus based shared decision-making plan for the district, assure that said plan incorporated diversity and multicultural guarantees, assure that said plan incorporates in service needs, and begin the implementation of said plan."

The remaining administrator, Elgie Clucas, generally supported the superintendent. She often nodded affirmatively as he began to speak, possibly a signal of attention and deference to the bureaucratic position of the superintendent, but easily taken by those intent on a dialogical form of decision making as a sign of premature agreement, and as an unconscious deference to bureaucratic authority. Since their ideal was one of dialogic authority in which people were supposed to transcend their roles, this nodding may well have appeared as collusion. However, unlike Smith, the assistant principal, she had had actual experience with SBDM in another district, did not challenge its legality or legitimacy, and was much more accommodating.

The Discursive Dynamics of Bureaucratic and Dialogical Authority

There is, of course, an inherent ambiguity in deliberations of this kind, one that must straddle the official authority granted to officers such as school administrators, and the requirement to widen the level and scope of participation. For example, at the first meeting most people expected the superintendent to take the initiative, and he did so by stating what he saw the tasks of the committee to be. He read the letter of understanding and reviewed the history of SBDM in the district. He was especially attracted by the policy statement drawn up by the previous superintendent, Jimmy Fox. Even if it had not been acted on by the board at the time, he liked its concreteness, although he did not affirm the special attention given to the business community in that document. Yet, whatever his stance toward SBDM or his predecessor's attempt to operationalize it into policy, he was performing his role as the head officer of the district, appointed by its representative body. Indeed, in 1991 the board tacitly made the decision that passing such a policy did not conduce to the "public good." As an administrator appointed by the board, Superintendent Williams was bound by the determinations of the "general good" made by this board, which had not spoken definitively on the issue.

Yet while he performed his role as a "trustee of the public good" with an eye toward what the board would ultimately accept, the content of his discourse often reflected the "real people" perspective. At this first meeting, he raised the issue of who was missing from the table. It was pointed out that there were no students, no one from the noncertified support staff union, no one from the community, and no one from a number—indeed most—of the elementary schools. He asked certain people to recruit these people, and in doing so, of course both affirmed his own role as the primary keeper of the public good and as the advocate of the real people and the ideal of widening participation. He ended the meeting by saying that they should meet monthly. The others agreed.

At the next meeting, Williams came back to the question of definition, but now invited the members of the group to participate in the activity of defining the meanings of the two terms, *site-based decision making* and *shared decision making*. People offered different definitions and at the end of going over different conceptions (e.g., management versus decision making, process versus outcome, inclusion), Williams attempted to summarize: "The idea is that decisions are made by those closest to those affected. The closer you are to the affected, the better the decision . . . I think that all of us have that notion in our heads." They then agreed that they should look at what already existed in the district and how people saw it and felt about it.

Williams also demonstrated his authority by leading the formation of a consensus around the issue of leadership itself. He said that he saw the need for "someone that's going to be our facilitator, the kind of person that's going to keep us all on track. I think that it would be important that we get someone who would help us solidify and clarify where we're going and that we're moving in the right direction and then start the discussion on how often we should meet and what our steps are." Another member of the committee asked untenured kindergarten teacher and PED member Marcy Bright if she would not like to volunteer to be the facilitator. She said no. Williams then said to her: "Would you consider, Marcy, and please say no if that's your inclination at this point. You have been very much involved with this Ed City Project for Democracy . . . educational democracy. You've kind of had your fingers in this pie, as it were, probably a bit longer than some of the others. Are you at all interested if there were people here that would put your name forward?"

Marcy Bright began to reflect out loud, and made reference to a problem that always plagues attempts to recruit people into participatory roles when they already have pressing obligations: "I'd be somewhat interested. I guess my main concern quite honestly is that I have a room full of somewhat needy students, and I honestly feel that I am not spending enough time there. So I guess it would depend on how much time it would take."

As the discussion proceeded, there developed a consensus for Bright to play such a role, but the committee members also understood her hesitancy—she had a reputation for being an excellent teacher who was devoted to her pupils. So she was asked if she would be more inclined to accept the facilitator position if someone agreed to share it with her. Three people volunteered: Assistant Principal Smith, who was resistant to the idea of SBDM, Elgie Clucas, the principal at the elementary school, and Rhonda Silver, the high school teacher who regularly contested Superintendent Williams's claim that the district already had SBDM.

The superintendent once again exerted bureaucratic authority even as he validated a certain level of equality. He said that he liked the idea of the high school teacher serving as co-facilitator along with Marcy Bright, and he explained his reasons:

> I kind of like the notion that we as administration, are important members of this committee, but we're not facilitators. I don't have any reason for that other than it sometimes appears from the outside that we're . . .

Someone finished his sentence for him, "That you have a silent agenda." He went on,

> Yeah, that we have one and that we're pushing it, or that we have it going in a direction that we want it to go in. So I like the notion of you two [teachers] co-chairing or co-facilitating. You're elementary and secondary. You both work intimately with students. You both have a sense or a notion of what site-based decision making is all about. So I would be very comfortable, I'm speaking again as one person here, with you two kind of co-chairing it and of course anything that we could do to help with running things off, with getting people in places for us to talk to, etc. I mean I could be helpful moving people.

Thus in validating equality among the members of the committee, even one who challenges his definitions, the superintendent also affirms that he is the validator.

Bureaucrats within a Dialogical Setting

Of course, the superintendent was not speaking as just one person among equals. Once he spoke, it was unlikely that his administrative subordinates were going to continue to say that they would serve as co-facilitators. On the one hand, the superintendent's statement was meant to convey the idea that he was not using his bureaucratic authority to determine the outcome, that he was merely one person among equals on the committee. Indeed, he was giving up the directive role that he assumed at the first session. On the other hand, the other administrators would clearly take this as a signal to go along. Or, to put the ambiguity a little differently, sometimes dialogical authority needs a little bureaucratic shove.

Both legitimacy and the appearance of legitimacy were at stake in this little "moving of people." He did not want it to appear that the administration was using its authority to determine the process and the outcome of the committee's functioning. It is no suggestion of duplicity to think that he might also have been concerned that the choice of one of the other administrators in such a role could have led to discord among the administrators themselves, or lowered the standing of one while raising that of the other.

His move also distanced the administration somewhat should the committee's work incur the disapproval of the school board. Thus, it provided a layer of protection for the continuing and future exercise of his authority in other areas. So it is probable that there was a mix of motives—not wanting to appear as covertly directing the operation and protecting the bureaucracy and its authority in the eyes of the board—in the superintendent's signaling his subordinates to take back their offer to serve as co-facilitators. Thus, even in this setting where everyone understands the significance of dialogical authority, bureaucratic considerations are still an important component in the deliberations.

We do not know whether these thoughts were consciously in the forefront of the superintendent's mind when he decided not to support the selection of one of the two administrators as a facilitator, but his decision and his behavior were consistent with the bureaucratic needs of his office. And they conformed perfectly with Robert A. Dahl's classical definition of power: one actor getting others to do what they otherwise would not have done, in this case withdrawing their names from consideration as a committee facilitator.[9]

Participatory Democrats Within a Bureaucratic Setting

The episode raises a concern that had been first expressed within the PED itself when it was suggested that both administrators and board

---

9. Robert A. Dahl, "The Concept of Power," *Behavioral Science* 2, 3 (1957): 201–215. "A has power over B to the extent that he can get B to do something that B would not otherwise do," 202–203.

members should be invited to attend the community meetings. At that time, those arguing that they should won out. William Purcell, the kindergarten teacher who would subsequently lead the successful campaign to change the character of school board elections, and who had been central to the PED's very early efforts, argued that this posed a danger that the administrators and the board members would not be able to separate out their roles and participate as just one among many equals. Purcell largely stopped coming to the PED meetings after he lost on the issue. However, the difficulty that he was alluding to is reflected in this interaction within the district committee and the necessary but uncomfortable interplay of bureaucratic and dialogical authority.

Neither Marcy Bright nor Rhonda Silver, the co-facilitating teachers, were inhibited by the presence of the administration. We found out at one of the committee meetings that Marcy came from the same city and neighborhood and was educated, albeit in a different age cohort, in the same parochial school as the superintendent. This shared background seemed to give Joe Williams a certain ease with Bright. On the other hand, the relationship between Williams and Silver was more tense. As already indicated, Silver, tenured and with many years of experience in the district, directly and continuously contradicted his contention that the district already had SBDM. She contended, rather, that the district was governed in a top-down bureaucratic manner, by the school board and the administration. Silver had earlier argued alongside Purcell when he warned that it would be impossible for administrators to separate out their roles if they entered the process. But it should be noted that Silver had also voiced to us concerns about the bureaucratic tendencies of unions and about how those tendencies also could affect the PED with its close ties to the union. And indeed, partly because of an illness but also partly out of a certain skepticism of the union/PED relationship, Silver, while participating in the PED community meetings, kept more of a distance from the PED than did Bright who was on the PED's steering/coordinating committee.

But within the context of the district committee meetings, Bright as well as Silver maintained some distance from the PED. They referred to the PED as "it" rather than "we" and presented themselves as representatives of neither the union nor the PED but as teachers who were trying to fulfill the mandate of the letters of understanding, that is, implement the agreement mandated by contractual authority by beginning the process of rendering the system more inclusively democratic. But just as there was an ambiguity in the roles of the administrators, so it was not easy for them to separate out their roles as district committee members, union members, and PED participants. Indeed, the work of the district committee did have some negative effects on the PED.

The PED began as an oppositional reform movement uncomfortable with representational/bureaucratic authority, even if it was not willing to go as far William Purcell wanted to in excluding administrators and board members from its community meetings. However, in connecting to the district committee this oppositional character was severely tested. This is reflected in the different comportment of the two district committee co-facilitators, who came from the PED.

Marcy Bright's reaction to the confrontation between her colleague and the superintendent is interesting because it represents a different vision of the relationship of the agent of change to the established institutional authority. She felt caught between two very strong antagonists, and found the meetings painful when they contested each other. She felt that mistrust was detracting from the committee's task of finding a new and more inclusive and democratic way to govern the schools.

As the district committee was functioning, the PED itself began to meet less and less frequently and lose vitality. Bright saw the numbers dwindling and the PED itself no longer doing as much as it had. In the midst of the conflict between Silver and the superintendent, she came to one of the PED meetings and questioned whether or not the PED should even continue to meet at all. Indeed, it seemed to us as well that the functioning of the district committee had absorbed tremendous time and both physical and emotional energy and taken much of the wind out of the PED's sails.

The difference between Bright's and Silver's response and the dwindling energy of the PED as it entered into a more cooperative relation with the established institutional authority raises the question of just how far cooperation can go without becoming co-optation. It was this question and the difficulty in answering it that implicitly was behind the different ways in which the two teachers—Rhonda Silver, a veteran of civil rights and anti-Vietnam war struggles, a person who had been disillusioned by the fate of earlier attempts at school reform within the district, and Marcy Bright, a young teacher and former Peace Corps volunteer with still untarnished idealism—responded to the process in which they were both engaged.

CHAPTER SEVEN

Cooperation and Co-optation

The Issue of Purity

Groups opposed to the status quo often worry about diluting their message by entering the halls of power and finding themselves co-opted by larger forces and institutional and bureaucratic habits and interest. Such a concern has often been voiced by some members of the Project for Educational Democracy (PED). Yet for the most part, as its participation in the district committee suggests, the PED has been willing to enter into collaborative relations with the administration in the belief that such collaboration could advance their own ideals. While there has been some tension between individual members of the PED and individual administrators, they have often found themselves working together toward a goal that has been perceived to be common. Yet a number of change-orientated theorists continue to warn against such cooperation, believing that the powers that be are too powerful to sleep with and that the lambs must stay clear of the lions.

John Dryzek, for example, has argued that there is a very good reason for reform or oppositional movements within the civil society to stay out of the orbit of the state. This is because of the need to retain "a flourishing oppositional civil society [as] the key to further democratization."[1] Out of a fear of absorption by the state of social movements and the drying up of oppositional civil society, except in exceptional circum-

---

1. John S. Dryzek, "Political Inclusion and the Dynamics of Democratization," *The American Political Science Review* 90, 1 (September 1996): 486.

stances he urges groups within civil society to resist becoming enmeshed with state structures.[2]

The PED presents us with a test of Dryzek's concern. It is an oppositional group that has become involved with established power, initially by sending a delegation to meet with the superintendent on a monthly basis and then by increasing the investment of the time and energy of some of its key participants in the district committee process.

Given the severely lessened vitality of the PED itself after the district committee began to function, it is difficult to argue with Dryzek's point and its applicability to this case. But in a relatively small context where people know each other well and must continue to work together on a day to day basis, maintaining communication and building trust become important elements in any strategy for change. To be sure, this carries with it the risk that Dryzek points out. But within local settings a totally oppositional posture won't work because if one is truly dedicated to democracy there are two kinds of goals that must be kept in sight: the specific goals of inclusion or empowerment of the disempowered, and as much cohesiveness and trust as is possible in the community. For, as we pointed out in chapter 3, the PED is as much about community building as it is about democratization. In its view, one cannot have one without the other.

Authorities at Risk

Dryzek's analysis would be more persuasive if, to take the Ed City example, the PED were the only group placing itself and its form of authority (dialogical) at risk. However, there is a lot of risk to go around in the process and a lot of different forms of authority that have something to lose. Above we made reference to some of the more personal kinds of risks taken by people who served on the district committee, especially the risk of incurring the disfavor of people in superior positions. However, the analysis can go beyond the vulnerability of individual people and address the vulnerability of different modes of authority themselves.

In contractually agreeing to the formation of a district-wide committee on which sat PED members who had called for devolution of some of the school board's powers, the board was obviously placing its

---

2. The two circumstances are that the group's "defining interest can be assimilated to any state imperative" and "whether the group's entry into the state would leave behind a flourishing civil society" (484–485). Dryzek clearly thinks, which is the whole point of the article, that these two criteria will rarely be met.

representational authority at risk. The superintendent was placing his bureaucratic authority at risk insofar as the process obscured the chain of command, threatening to break into a dissociated and uncoordinated set of decision processes. It also threatened to reduce his control over the building principals as well as his ability to protect them from the effects of unpopular decisions. The PED's authority, especially its claim to be a genuine interpreter of the community's unarticulated will, particularly its excluded segments, was also at risk for two reasons. First, it was at risk because the members of the PED who were also serving on the district committee distanced themselves from the PED itself, serving as agents with independent voices, sometimes even differing between themselves. Second, the PED's idea about minority participation was most vigorously challenged by one of the few African Americans (Assistant Principal Smith) who sat on the district committee. Thus, the authority that the PED brought to the table on the basis of its attempts to mobilize and decipher the voice of the community, and particularly its excluded elements, were at risk in the district committee process. The union, and its contractual authority, was also at risk because if the process failed its insistence that the letters of understanding be appended to the contact would appear to have been much ado about nothing. The professional authority of teachers was also at risk should their autonomy over educational decisions be diminished.

The authority of the district committee was at risk as well. First, no one could know how the school board would receive the recommendations that were ultimately submitted to it by the district committee, if indeed the latter could agree on recommendations. Second, the district committee, which was mandated to investigate the degree of inclusivity and Site-Based Decision Making (SBDM) in the present system and to itself be inclusive of the different affected parties, was having difficulty recruiting the people it needed to be in compliance with the letter of understanding. The superintendent noted at the very first meeting that they would have to spread out and try to recruit others, and people there offered to work on bringing specific people in. But they had constant difficulty in recruiting and maintaining the presence of students.[3] Despite many efforts to inform parents of the meetings, few attended. A total of eight African Americans participated at one point or another over a two-

---

3. Rhonda Silver sometimes convinced two African American and one Arab high school student to attend some of the sessions, but the meetings often had no students present.

year period,[4] but with the exception of Assistant Principal Smith, who opposed turning over power to school councils, their attendance was scattered and of short duration. Moreover, with two exceptions,[5] the continuous members of the district committee were all institutionally tied to the system as administrators, teachers, or board members. So here we had a situation in which a committee that was supposed to be investigating degrees of inclusion in the present system and looking forward to new, more inclusive patterns of decision making could not make itself more inclusive in any satisfactory way. That fact did not escape the committee members. As they persisted in their work they constantly reminded themselves that they had to try to make *this* committee more inclusive.

The second letter of understanding that served as a charge to the district committee specified that it "develop a consensus based shared decision-making plan for the district, [and] assure that said plan incorporates diversity and multicultural guarantees." As we have just seen, the district committee was unable to diversify itself as it would have liked in order to serve as an exemplary model of the kind of inclusive process it wanted to stimulate in all of the schools. While homogeneity can sometimes increase the likelihood of a consensual mode of operation with minimal conflict, the risks due to differences in authoritative position that we have been discussing ensured that there would be conflict on the committee.

Cooperative Confrontation v. Strong Participation

Jane Mansbridge has created an ideal-type "unitary" model of democracy where members of a collectivity share both goals and a commitment to internal equality. But, she argues, in real life such groups are

---

4. Two decided to take college courses to improve their education and job prospects. They no longer had the time to participate. One came to one meeting in the late afternoon and said she found it difficult to get off from work. But even after the committee switched to evening meetings, she did not return. Kareem Saleem, the African American community organizer who was active in the PED, attended sometimes, but at other times his work obligations pulled him away and in one instance he said he just forgot, something that it is not difficult for very active and busy people to do. Another African American mother and president of the Parks School PTA came a couple of times and that was it.

5. One was the board member who continued to attend after he lost his seat in the 1997 elections, the other was Georgia Senn, the parent who came into the process in the second year of its operation and became the facilitator at the end of that year.

likely on occasion to fray and will need to learn how to shift back and forth between a unitary consensual mode of decision making and a conflictual majority-minority form where decisions are made by voting.[6] The district committee never allowed itself to be divided between a majority and a minority. It never took a vote. And it never completely overcame conflict. But the members never stopped talking in their determination to fulfill their mandate.

The process conformed more to Benjamin Barber's model of "strong" participatory democracy where conflict is an ever-present feature of the process than to Mansbridge's ideal type "unitary" model, which is a consensual process among those with "equal respect" and "equal status," or even to Mansbridge's more empirical examples of conflict under exceptional circumstances.[7] While at times the process looked as though it was going to self-destruct because of the level of conflict, somehow the participants always came to a realization that this would be the worst possible outcome for themselves and for those who were to be served by their work. They thus pushed ahead and developed a plan for a more inclusive and decentralized method of decision making within the schools. They did this by successfully managing the conflict that was either manifest or an ever-present possibility due to the ambiguities and risks associated with different and shifting authoritative positions. And they did it by talking the conflict through rather than by recourse to defeating the minority through a vote.

Mutual Co-optation of Authority

One of the underlying themes within the PED that continued in the district committee was the possibility of the co-optation of dialogical authority by bureaucratic or representative authority. The theme was first expressed at the PED community meeting where William Purcell argued unsuccessfully for the exclusion of administrators and board members from the PED, and it resurfaced during the district committee meetings in the constant faceoff between the superintendent and Rhonda Silver, and in Marcy Bright's discomfort with these exchanges.

When this theme was openly expressed by Silver, as it sometimes was in our discussions with her, it was always in terms of those in formal positions of authority coopting the energy of those below, and there

---

6. Mansbridge, chapter 20.
7. Ibid., 30.

were a number of times in the meetings of the district committee when this seemed to be occurring. When this happened it was not necessarily because of any ill will or conscious intent to deceive. Sometimes it occurred because of the kinds of networks that people in formal positions of authority frequently have—associations of like-minded people in similar positions of authority.

For example, after conducting a survey of attitudes toward the present system among teachers, parents, and students during its first year of existence,[8] in the second year they began a search for a model that could serve as a blueprint in the construction of a pilot program. Here the superintendent used his acquaintance with other superintendents in the state to help the district committee explore possible models of shared decision making that might be used. He contacted several districts to see if they would be willing to give a presentation and answer questions that district committee members might have. One district was willing to do this and sent a team composed of the superintendent of that district, an elementary school principal, a parent, a school counselor, and a school bus driver. Each of these people spoke enthusiastically of their system.

This district did differ in some characteristics from Ed City. It was spread out over a large rural area and included a number of small towns,

---

8. The survey of parents was conducted by telephone, which itself carries a racial/class skewing. Thus, it is not surprising that 13 percent of the parents responding were African American while 22.5 percent of the elementary school students in the district were African American in 1989–90. Parents reported low levels of participation in school decisions, a feeling that their opinions were not heard, a moderate satisfaction with the way that decisions were made in their children's schools, and a desire to participate more.

A separate written random survey of PTA parents provided quite indeterminate results—twenty-nine of the thirty-seven parents said that they are "moderately to very comfortable with the decisions made by the school which affect their child." However, twenty-six said that they "moderately or strongly disagreed that their concerns were respected by the school." A random written survey of high school students found very low rates of participation in the areas of courses and teaching methods, selection of faculty and staff, and building rules and policies, but a relatively even split when it came to the way money was spent in the building. In terms of certified staff (teachers), there was not a wide concurrence of perceptions over who made decisions. This reflected differences between schools. In general, there was an age split among teachers, with younger teachers being more satisfied and older teachers being less satisfied with the way decisions were made. But there was no really strong dissatisfaction registered. Noncertified staff reported little involvement in decision making and low levels of satisfaction with the decision-making processes.

none of which came even close to Ed City in population. It had virtually no African American children. Unlike Ed City it had a significant Latino population, but this population was concentrated in one area and one school and all of the people who visited the Ed City District were white. Therefore, this district had little to offer Ed City in terms of how SBDM might help to empower underrepresented minorities whose children were spread throughout the system.

In addition, this district had no systematic way of selecting people for participation on the decision-making committees. The parent said that anyone who came to complain to a principal became a ripe target for recruitment. The elementary school principal said that the responsibility for recruiting parents and community people was left to him and he approached city employees such as police officers and firefighters.

Although there was a considerable difference between this district's ideas of shared decision making and those initially articulated by members of the PED, the differences were largely overlooked, at least initially, as everyone grasped for ways to implement the idea of site-based or shared decision making. Indeed, the "or" here is important because while the visiting district had some form of SBDM it did not have the same kind of inclusive shared decision making that the PED had sought. While eventually the district committee would refocus on this issue, the meetings immediately following the visitors' presentation were taken up with the practical question of which school would be the pilot that would select people for training in decision making.

Unpacking the Concept of Co-optation

The above segment is useful for understanding a part of the concept of co-optation. In the above episode considerations of basic purposes and aims are displaced by considerations of feasibility. In this case, the superintendent's expertise in the form of a large professional network was able to supply the committee members with a concrete exemplar of a functioning site-based system. However, the ambiguity of the concept of SBDM hid, at least momentarily, the fact that this exemplar did not have the same kind of diversity that Ed City has and it lacked any consistent criteria for recruiting people to the decision-making bodies. And because it is not ethnically and racially diverse in the same way that Ed City is, it was not confronting the same kind of inclusivity issue that Ed City was.

There is another element of "co-optation" that is revealed in this episode. Networks of people are imbedded in ideological frameworks in which people respond in similar manners to certain problems. This means that there is a tendency to define problems in certain standardized ways as well as to develop solutions that are constrained in certain ways. There was, in this case, a certain understandable comfort that the Ed City superintendent gained by knowing that his counterpart could live with that system. That element tended to make that system an acceptable model and to exclude other possibilities where the degree of comfort was absent or uncertain. Yet "co-optation" is a loaded term, often indicating a more conscious attempt to fool and implying a kind of innocence on the part of the fooled.

In fact the entire district committee did learn from this visit. One of the lessons that was reinforced by the visitors was the importance of training. All people who participate in their shared decision-making bodies go through intensive training. Initially, that district had contracted out with a professional training program in consensus decision making in educational contexts. After several years of experience with SBDM, they undertook their own training, and they offered to train people in Ed City as well.

It was largely as a result of this offer, and of the school board's wanting to see a specific proposal, that the district committee felt pressed to move quickly toward the development of a pilot project, or plural projects. Superintendent Williams pushed to have a single pilot project in the elementary school where Clucas, a member of the district committee, was principal. There was considerable disagreement on the committee over whether this should be the only project. Williams appeared to get his way, but Clucas reported back to the district committee that when she tried to interest teachers in volunteering for the training, she got nowhere. She said that she had willing parents, but no willing teachers. In the meantime, the district that had offered to train Ed City's people withdrew its offer, saying that it could not be prepared to train that early after all. For a while the prospects for broadly shared SBDM in Ed City dimmed.

Co-optation and Independent Players

If purists argue that PED was coopted by the district committee, nonpurists might counter that the district committee was also co-opted by the PED and its participatory ideology, and that this left room for new independent players to emerge.

For example, feeling that the district committee had dropped the ball, Adele Stein, the former president of the teachers union and key initiator of the PED who had since become an elementary school principal herself, pushed ahead with the constitution of shared decision-making committees in her own school, Steer School. There, it will be recalled, teachers had a long tradition of making decisions by committee but parents and community people were excluded. So Stein was making more inclusive an already existing participatory process. The contrast is interesting because while the principal on the district committee was reporting that teachers were not interested and that perhaps the union needed to do more to get them interested, Stein, working within the very different Steer School culture, was moving full speed ahead. And, not having been a party to the district committee meetings, she was acting outside of its authority. The advantage, of course, was that, ironically, she was able to use her own bureaucratic authority to move things along without waiting for anyone's approval. The disadvantage was that she did not have the authorization to serve as a model for the district and hence her successes and her failures might turn out to be Steer's alone, just as Steer had for years stood alone in its system of participatory decision making by its teachers.

Although a number of the participants on the district committee admired her breakthrough during a particularly pessimistic period of the committee's work (both the training offer and the single "official" pilot program falling through), most saw it as posing a threat to the authority of the district committee and to the construction of a district-wide system of inclusion. Thus, when Adele Stein went to the district committee for a share of the money that was to be allocated for training, the district committee, over the objection of teacher/PED member Rhonda Silver, refused, saying that since she was operating outside of the district-wide framework she would have to get her training money elsewhere. But the district committee had no authority to stop her and Joe Williams was unwilling to use his authority as superintendent to attempt to do so. Indeed, was this not one more example of the "site-based stuff" that he had been arguing, against Silver, was going on in the district?

Thus, while there was one school that was breaking out in front of the rest, with the principal using her authority at the local school site to do so, it was seen by most of the district committee members as a kind of renegade operating outside of the district-wide process that their committee was working on, and thus outside of the spirit of the contractual agreement insisted on by the union of which Stein was president before assuming the principalship of Steer School! Stein had grown impatient with the district committee process and pessimistic that it would lead anywhere. But her PED colleagues on the committee were still trying to make it work, and to find a model that the district committee could agree on, à la the letters of understanding between the board and the teachers' union. Here we can see how incredibly fuzzy lines of authority can become and how the processes of co-optation can flow in multiple directions.

Co-optation of Existing Structures to Advance Progressive Ends

At the end of a particularly frustrating and acrimonious meeting, Marcy Bright recalled that the visitors who had come to explain their system had said that it was built upon an already existing process, the School Improvement process that was mandated for every school in the state by the state board of education. The state legislature used its representative authority to mandate regular school assessments. The state board of education, appointed by the elected governor, used its bureaucratic authority to stipulate that there had to be a specific process whereby schools would evaluate their own performances and make proposals for self-improvement. And such a process had to involve more than just a single person, the principal, determining and writing up the plan.

The district that had offered to train Ed City participants in SBDM had used this legislative and bureaucratic mandate to legitimize and structure their SBDM system. Bright proposed, and the district committee accepted, the idea of doing the same thing in Ed City. Thus, they would be expanding the authority and making more inclusive bodies on which teachers, *by state mandate*, were already expending time and energy.[9] This undercut the earlier contention made by the assistant principal that the direction in which the committee was going violated the school code. At this point, the administrators on the committee became more positive and began to join in and work with the idea. The assistant principal went along, and Clucas, who had reported no success in recruiting teachers for training allowed that she could not have chosen a worse time, the end of the spring semester, when teachers were already

---

9. In fact, for three years prior to this the only African American principal in the system had brought parents and community people into advisory committees within the School Improvement process. But as at Steer School, it was ultimately the teachers assembled who made the decisions. The principal made her preferences known but never overruled the decision of the teachers. If people on the district committee knew of this, they did not reveal it at the committee meetings.

feeling overloaded. Under the new plan, teachers in most of the schools would likely have new areas of decision making to deal with, but they would not be faced with an additional layer of responsibility over and above the already existing School Improvement committees. Bright had thus found a way to co-opt the bureaucratic authority of the superintendent and the representative authority of the state. She used the model that the superintendent was comfortable with, and she appealed to the representative and bureaucratic authority of the state, which mandated the process, to appease the concerns of other administrators and to advance the aims of dialogical authority.

But there is a curious déjà vu twist to the story. Having agreed on the legitimizing use of the School Improvement process, the district committee set itself to drafting its recommendations. As we have already indicated, Superintendent Williams reviewed the ill-fated, very detailed policy statement offered by his predecessor back in 1991 and liked its specificity and concreteness. He knew that the controversy surrounding it was due largely to the bad blood existing between his predecessor and the school board. But Joe Williams had an excellent relationship with the board, and thought that the document itself was solid.[10]

All members of the district committee seemed to agree. A subcommittee was appointed and used the earlier document to produce a draft proposal that specified nine areas in which School Improvement team members would be trained. It also included specification on the process for selection of members, the composition of the teams or committees, and the functions of committee facilitators and secretaries. One copy of the report was sent to each school so that teachers would have a chance to read it. It was also presented to a meeting of the superintendent's "cabinet," that is, the principals and assistant superintendents.

Midlevel Change and Problems of Accountability and Authority

Two principals who had not participated in the district committee process showed up in person at a subsequent meeting of the district committee to respond to the draft while another had a letter read at the next district committee meeting. All three argued that the committee report was too detailed and that there had to be greater flexibility given to each of the schools to accommodate their particular circumstances.

---

10. Indeed, the board was in the process of putting together a very large salary increase because it had learned that another district was trying to attract him away.

In an attempt to gain a consensus and to not be seen as a part of a coercive centralized bureaucratic arm itself, the committee got rid of many of the specifications and changed much of the obligatorily directive language ("will") to more conditionally persuasive language ("may" and "ideally will").

Superintendent Williams, who as we have seen had favored the more directive language, said that the softening of the language notwithstanding, he would use his authority to make sure that each school would take the mandate of inclusivity seriously and take concrete measures to achieve it. At the last meeting of the district committee, which neither the superintendent nor the principal on the committee could attend, there was a discussion as to whether the committee would disband or whether it would come together again in a year to assess what progress had been made. All but Smith, the only administrator present, agreed that they would reconvene. He argued that the committee's mandate was over. Someone else said that this was Joe Williams's view as well. Georgia Senn, the parent who had taken over as facilitator from Silver and Bright in the final year of the committee's work, saw that Smith was unhappy. When she expressed concern to Smith over his obvious consternation, he replied: "Look, I don't want you to think that because I said what I thought, that I don't accept the consensus of the committee." Smith clearly saw that this was in the overall interest of community as well as committee harmony, a goal that he shared with the others. Once again, there were conflicting ideas but no adversarial vote.

The parent and teacher members of the district committee felt that while they had been able to reach a compromise consensus and create the possibility for a more inclusive participatory reform of the district, that outcome was not at all certain. So they made one more decision, which was that it was absolutely essential to revitalize the PED both to help recruit people from previously excluded categories and to serve as a movement outside of the system to monitor the concrete performance of the schools.

But if it is rejuvenated, it will be difficult for the PED to frame its activity around the devolutionary language of the pre–district committee years. Its sight will have to be focused on inclusion at each of the local schools, with perhaps periodic intrusion into the electoral process to promote the presence of minorities on the school board. For while it was extremely rare for parents or community people to be included on bodies actually making decisions in the individual schools, there was still a good bit of autonomy all along on the precise decision-making processes in them. It was this that superintendent Williams was referring to when he said that there was a good bit of SBDM within the system. He may now find himself intruding more into those processes if principals use the less specifically directive language in the committee report in order to complacently justify the exclusion of parents and community members, especially minority people.

But it appears that it will not just be left to the superintendent, or to the district committee members who refused to permanently disband, or to the PED if it indeed can be revitalized. Sara Holmes, the PED member who had won a seat on the school board, had been a member of the district committee. She also served on the district's equity committee. This was a committee of a much shorter duration than the district committee, which was appointed by the board to make specific policy proposals to remedy the shortcomings detected by both the Office of Civil Rights and the district's own commissioned equity audit. Shortly after the decision of the district committee members to reconstitute themselves in a year to assess the remedial progress made by the district, Holmes successfully proposed that the equity committee do the same thing.

Both committees are concerned with the inclusion of African American and less affluent citizens in educational decision making. It will be interesting to see if bodies which had been initially legitimized by representational, contractual, and/or bureaucratic authority to accomplish a certain task can continue to extend their own authority and legitimacy in the eyes of the public in order to hold the system accountable. This would be different from the PED, which operates purely in the domain of civil society without ever having had a grant of authority from formal representative or administrative bodies. The best analogy to the extension of these two committees might be found in the international domain, Non Governmental Organizations (NGOs) recognized as performing important operations by the United Nations but remaining autonomous in their powers and operations. This actually comes very close to the blurring of the complex of state and autonomous but authoritative bodies advocated by Paul Hirst in his book *Associative Democracy*.[11] The appearance of the PED in the public sphere of Ed City has given rise to a very interesting political and educational laboratory.

The Mirror Image of Co-optation

Those who work for fundamental change by refusing any engagement with established authority will find their mirror image in the very

---

11. Paul Hirst, *Associative Democracy* (Amherst: University of Massachusetts Press, 1994).

bureaucracy that they fear. Their concern about co-optation by the bureaucracy is echoed within the bureaucracy by those who regard accountability through the chain of command as the primary value. While the former are concerned about any process that waters down their vision, the latter are concerned about any process that waters down their responsibility, believing that it is untenable to hold administrators responsible for decisions made by unaccountable bodies. This position was expressed in the PED by William Purcell when he stopped coming to PED meetings after unsuccessfully arguing that board members and administrators should not be invited to their meetings. It was also expressed in the district committee meetings by Sidney Smith and other administrators who feared that to give control over to a collaborative body was to abdicate responsibility for the running of the school.

Both Purcell and Smith were expressing a concern for clarity and purity of function. For the reformer it is for purity of purpose. For the administrator it is for purity of accountability. It is important that the value of these concerns be acknowledged. After all, Purcell went on to lead a major election reform even while members of the PED were working within the system to advance higher levels of participation. And, as we saw, one very prominent African American group agreed strongly with Smith's point of view that lines of accountability must be clear if teachers and administrators are to take responsibility for their children's education, indicating that direct participation is not always the goal of all members of PED's target groups.

Yet while these are mirrored images of each other, they are not the same, and the lines are not always so easy to maintain. For example, Purcell removed himself from the PED after arguing that the inclusion of board members and administrators would threaten the participatory process. Exclusion was the price that had to be paid for greater inclusion. And Smith, by acquiescing to those parents, community members, and teachers on the district committee who sought to extend their mandate and monitor the process, went along with the blurring of institutionalized lines of accountability and responsibility.

These contradictions suggest that purity is itself rarely fully realizable in the concrete world of social action. It is not, however, to suggest that the concern for accountability, responsibility, and clarity of purpose are unimportant. We return to these issues in the concluding chapter.

CHAPTER EIGHT

Conclusion: Competing Conceptions of Democratic Education and Theory

From Systems Level Devolution to Midlevel Change

In this book, we have explored the work of the Project for Educational Democracy (PED). We began by describing its visions for a more democratic school system and then we examined the evolution of this vision as some of its internal tensions became apparent and as the PED came into contact with other groups with different agendas and alternative conceptions of educational governance. In this chapter we want to return to the name that the PED gave itself, the Project for *Educational Democracy,* and explore the way in which those terms modify one another. For not all democracy is educational and not all education is democratic. We believe that other communities can learn from the work of the PED and the way in which it drew these terms together into a community-based movement. And we also believe that the work of the PED can inform both political and educational theory.

There are three levels of decision making in the typical public school district. The first is the all-system level. The school board and the superintendent's office occupy this level and to various degrees set the parameters for what goes on at all other levels. The second or middle level is the individual school itself. Typically, school-wide decisions are made by the school principal. Finally, there is the classroom. Normally teachers have wide latitude, often referred to as "teacher autonomy," to decide on the conduct of the educational process within their own classrooms.

The district committee has proposed community participation in the decision making of every school. The change is best viewed as a middle-level reform in the sense that the primary site for change is the individual school. The committee is not offering system-wide reform or classroom reform, although both may be outcomes arising from the inclusion of members of the community in decisions about individual schools. Whatever its wider impact, the change is a middle-level reform because it is bounded by the command structure that is the school board and the superintendent on top and the classroom teacher below. It does not directly relate to decisions that must be made on the system level, such as the school calendar, where to set the boundaries of the individual school attendance area, when and where to build a new school, or when to close an older one. Of course, a more coherent body of parents and community members at the level of the individual school may have a greater influence on these decisions, but decisions such as these are ultimately determined at the system level.

This is particularly interesting because when the PED began, its discourse was a system-level discourse. It must be remembered that the PED began after a bitter strike and difficult negotiation with the school board, that it saw the all-white and at that time middle-class and largely academic board as insensitive to the needs of African American children, and that its rhetoric about "reclaiming" the schools was taken by the board with some reason as meaning at least in part "from them." The other part was also system-level, the administration. While some of the criticisms of the status quo in the PED's community meetings were directed against specific teachers, most involved criticisms of the way that the board and/or the administration was functioning.

The members of the PED who participated in the district committee process went in with the expectation that the process would involve system-level change. However, the discussions took an almost imperceptible turn toward change at the mid- or school level. In fact, Superintendent Williams was quite right when he said that there was lots of "site-based stuff" going on in the district, in that there was quite a variety of ways in which decisions were made in each of the schools. Some principals were very authoritarian and made almost all of the decisions themselves. Some involved teachers and in some limited cases parents and business partners, in a purely advisory capacity. One school, in addition to Steer, enhanced the power of teachers and the principal gave up veto authority. So, according to the definition that Superintendent Williams implicitly accepted when he tried to define Site Based Decision Making (SBDM), it already existed to a great extent in the district. But much of it was unknown to the PED when it began its push for system-wide change.

Even so, what did not exist was a systematic policy whereby parents and community people, and at the high and middle schools, students, had a say in the actual making of school decisions. When the district committee turned to the School Improvement process to accomplish this, it in fact found a middle-level solution. There was no devolution of power from the school board involved. The decisions were already being made at the school level. And, ironically, it came as very welcome news on the district committee when the superintendent said that he would use his higher bureaucratic authority to make certain that the School Improvement committees made every effort to reflect the diversity of parents and community members.

The proposed reforms are also middle level because they do not address classroom practice even though that is where some of the most serious disparities occur or at least originate, for instance, disparities in the evaluation of student performance and discipline. It leaves open to negotiation just how a higher level of participation will affect the day to day work of teachers in the classroom, but it does not mandate any change by itself. We suspect that one of the reasons that the PED never generated widespread enthusiasm among a large segment of the teacher population is not only because of the time demanded by its meetings and planning sessions, but also because teachers perceive themselves as autonomous within the classroom. Indeed, this perception is one of the attractive aspects of teaching. "The pay may not be great, but once the classroom door is closed, I am my own boss." And one African American teacher who attended a PED meeting openly voiced a concern that she might be subject to the control of largely white middle- and upper-class parents under conditions of a greater nonprofessional say in the running of the schools.

Given the recent turn toward testing and accountability, the desire for strong autonomy is being challenged, and a more cooperative stance between the teaching staff and the community may be required to mitigate the more adverse effects of rigid test accountability. Much like so-called "truth in sentencing laws," discretion is taken away from the person best trained to exercise it, and the only way to return it may be to create greater trust, dialogue, and working relationships between the professional and the community. We do not necessarily agree with those who hold that there is an inevitable split between the role of the professional and the role of the community. A closer relationship between teacher and community may bring about greater respect for the judgment of the teacher and less reliance on overinterpreted test results. "Autonomy" cannot any longer be taken to mean hermetically sealed off from parental or community concerns.

Nor can democracy be taken simply to mean "ALL power to the people" at the expense of educated professionals. The task is to find ways of facilitating communication and participation, while at the same time recognizing limits on intrusion by nonprofessionals. This was, in fact, one of the major issues put before the PED several times by union Director Jerry Mann who saw the commitment to shared/SBDM and teacher autonomy not as irreconcilable opposites, but as two positive values that had to be mediated through democratic participatory processes.

But what about the legal and bureaucratic accountability of the line administrators that Assistant Principal Smith was so concerned about on the district committee? In other words, is it unfair and unreasonable to hold administrators responsible for implementing decisions over which they have but minimum control? This concern was expressed in the district committee by both Assistant Principal Smith, the only continuously participating African American on the committee, and by the People for Educational Justice. This is a group of African Americans who believe that unless there is a clear hierarchical line of accountability, from child to teacher, to principal, to superintendent, no one will take responsibility for their children's education. Those on the district committee who were concerned about accountability feared that to give control over to a collaborative body would be to abdicate professional responsibility for the running of the school.

The legal issues initially raised by Smith were settled when the district committee saw they could use the state-mandated School Improvement committees, but for some the moral issue also raised by Smith remained. They did not object to an advisory role for parents and community members, but they had more problems with investing them with decision-making authority. From their point of view, schools must be responsible for the success or failure of students, and this requires strong personal accountability. Committee members can usually duck responsibility. The buck never stops in a committee.

We believe that this concern may miss some important points. First, there is no reason why principals cannot be held accountable, among other things, for the effective running of the committees themselves. Certainly there are communities so polarized politically that few schools would be able to maintain a reasonable educational climate through a committee structure. However, there is little evidence that without community support a reasonable educational climate can be maintained under other structures in such situations. Given reasonable safeguards against corruption and nepotism, factors that were never at issue in Ed City, there is some hope that more collaborative relations with the community could reestablish some of the trust that public schools have lost. This is a matter for empirical research, but there are two different kinds of questions that researchers might ask. The first is whether wider participation in school decisions improves education. The second, and we believe more important question, is, What are the factors that allow wider participation in school decision making to, first, enhance the legitimacy of public schools and, second, improve education?

Whichever of these questions is asked and however they may be answered, there is a conceptual tension in the idea of participation. The tension involves the question of whether the shape of participation is to be dictated from above (i.e., in a nonparticipatory way, as people believed former Superintendent Fox had wanted to do and as three principals felt the original draft report of the district committee would also have done), or whether the character of participation is to be determined from within each school itself, on the order of Steer School's going its own way before the district committee process was even completed. Some believe that determination from a strong leader at the superintendent's level can bypass the entrenched interests in the local schools and require participation from the previously excluded. Others object that this process is undemocratic and that change must arise from within each school itself with participation taking different forms from school to school.

Democratic theorists sometimes think in either/or terms. Either democracy has to be imposed from above (for the sake of unity, accountability, rights, equality, and knowledge) or from below (for the sake of self-determination, recognition of diversity of people and conditions, and the moral and cognitive development of participants). If it is imposed from above, the very process of its formation is undemocratic. Yet in reality, many different things are going on at the same time, and the idea that democracy is just one thing that happens in just one place at a time is misleading. When the district committee finally undertook to address this issue, it determined, after considerable feedback from principals, to allow more discretion on the part of individual schools about where, when, and how to institute parental and community participation in decision making. There are no guarantees in any social or political process, and as of this writing it is too early to compare the processes in individual schools. But the fact that both Superintendent Williams and members of the district committee decided to monitor but not to micromanage that process, may prove to be a crucial mediating position that will help to avoid some of the problems that Superintendent Fox ran into.

The PED's Accomplishments

Even though the change process took the middle-level course not anticipated by the PED at the beginning, there is still an impressive record of accomplishment. One of the exceptional features of the PED was precisely that it opened up a space where African American and white people, parents and teachers, system insiders and community people, and students and adults, could meet over a shared agenda. The PED's community meetings may have been the only place in the community where such meetings were held on a regular basis and where members of one group could actually check the perceptions and learn about the life experiences of members of the other. Thus, teachers could hear from the African American parents just how unfriendly the school felt to them when they visited it, or how slighted they felt when they were not informed of their children's problems or needs. And, after an initial disagreement over the issue, administrators were invited into this process of tapping nonprofessional sentiments as well.

The PED provided a structure that enabled people from different parts of the community to enter into a discussion about the future of public education in which the voice of a minority community was amplified. With this structure in place differences did not disappear, but many potentially contentious issues could be addressed around the table in a way that enabled more refined judgments to be made. An African American parent could tell teachers why she wanted stricter discipline for her third grader (because she feared that without the discipline African American children would be expelled by the seventh grade and imprisoned before they reached the end of high school); another could tell teachers that they felt that in-service training was taking too large a bite out of classroom time; teachers could explain the importance of in-service work for teacher development and performance and tell critical parents why they thought allowing teachers to split the kindergarten shift was a good idea (because, among other things, it helps retain high quality teachers); a community person, in charge of an Urban League boys program could discuss with both teachers and parents how to deal with class clowns (i.e., those who "act out" using humor are usually bright and creative, so try to rechannel these qualities); and students could offer their views of status differentials between schools to all of the adults. Given the scale of the PED and the problems associated with race in the United States, these episodes may seem like small drops in a sea of racial miscommunication and distrust. But encounters like these might well turn out to be the critical first steps for the development of strong working relationships between a school and its community.

Without such encounters distrust can be left to fester, and with it new wounds can easily be opened up. As we saw, some parents just felt unwelcome in the school, believing that the staff saw them as intruders who did not belong. Some of those who felt this way believed that there might be rather simple solutions, a comfortable waiting room with coffee for parents to sit in, or a different attitude on the part of staff and teachers. Cultural contact will not, of course, always result in agreement. It may sometimes result in more informed disagreement. And sometimes it may result in a significant level of structural change, as it did when William Purcell decided to lead his campaign to change the way the school board was elected.

We should not leave the impression that all that is required to refine judgment and advance democratic education is good will and community participation. For one thing the percentage of people in a community who are able to participate in a robust way at any given time is always small, and those participating in the PED are certainly the exception. Yet over time the availability of participatory structures allows people who may well be inclined to participate in community life to do so, even if intermittently or on one particularly meaningful occasion. There had already been considerable interest in questions of racial equity in the public schools on the part of African American groups (such as the PEJ, the Urban League, the NAACP, and the Ministerial Alliance), well before the PED began to operate. But what the PED added to this was the joint participation of the marginalized and excluded and of the professionals and the advantaged in its own deliberations, and a call for the marginalized and excluded to be included in the official decision making process. In addition, the PED, the district and equity committees, and the referendum movement to change the way of electing the school board (stimulated by William Purcell who had initially been mobilized by the PED) provided the community and its schools with a lot of what Robert Putman calls "social capital."[1] People have come out of their private domestic spheres to join publicly in support of a vision of what the public schools should be like.

It is well to remember, however, that participatory groups always work within framework norms and values that transcend the local structures in which they work, and it often helps to be working in tandem with larger external enforcement mechanisms. Thus, the achievements of

---

1. Robert D. Putnam, *Making Democracy Work: Civic Traditions in Modern Italy* (Princeton: Princeton University Press, 1993).

the PED must also be understood within the context of larger national themes and institutions and the way in which they impacted Ed City.

The outside pressure, coming well after both the PED and the district committee had been operating, included the findings of the Civil Rights Division of the U.S. Department of Education and the very real threat by an African American activist to file suit before the federal courts. When the PED began, there was a felt need on the part of both PED participants and others in the African American community to do something about what they perceived as serious inequities and exclusions. But there was no significant sense of crisis on the part of most of the members of the all-white school board. By the time that the Office of Civil Rights weighed in, the external auditors' findings were made public, and the threat of court action was presented to the board, there was much more of a crisis mentality. This mentality encouraged a more determined engagement by those already involved and brought more people into civic action around public education.

While strategies might differ, the common thread is more inclusiveness, and more participation. While the PED cannot claim credit for the appearance of other initiatives that arose during its functioning, the PED's vision of participation within the schools might well benefit from all these new entrants into the world of public education. After all, only seven people can sit on the school board at one time, but all of the elementary schools and the high and middle schools will have committees on which those previously outside the system could participate.

We have already made the case that the uniqueness of the PED lies in its inclusion of system insiders and outsiders. But it was not easy to sustain the participation of the people who were not actually working within the system. Indeed, even most teachers remained outside the PED.

The Future

The PED's vision of itself has been that of a grass roots community of interested people in public education not subject to any external authority other than the will of the people who choose to respond to its calls to meet and discuss issues of concern to them. Compared with the district and equity committees, which were constituted by formal external authorities and asked to make specific sorts of recommendations to the school board, the PED is certainly amorphous and carries with it all the problems of a group whose members have different experiences and levels of knowledge necessitating constant repetition and orientation for newcomers. But it also offers the greatest degree of freedom for dialogue. In any case, the membership of these two committees is fixed and it makes sense to limit it to those who have worked on the reports. The PED's membership has been open and self-selective. It has attracted people with very different experiential and knowledge bases. It has dealt with them as legitimate articulators of their own perceptions and interests, either as individuals or as members of underrepresented minorities. And it has proved to be a formative experience for a number of people who have had a concrete impact.

For example, experience in the PED motivated Sara Holmes to run successfully for the school board and to play such a crucial role in both the district committee and the equity committee. It also provided Edith Jones, the African American woman who appeared before the school board and was offended by the way she was "looked at," with a space to discuss educational issues before she made her own try for a seat on the board. Experience in the PED led young and inexperienced teacher Marcy Bright to become a very effective co-facilitator of the district committee and to break the deadlock on the district committee by suggesting utilization of the School Improvement committees to bring about greater inclusion. It also led Rhonda Silver to become a co-facilitator despite her disappointments with past reform efforts in the district. It was experience in the PED that led Georgia Senn, a parent, to assume the role of facilitator of the district committee in its last year of functioning when it had become too much for Rhonda Silver and Marcy Bright. Experience in the PED led Adele Stein, once she became principal of Steer School, to extend its participatory governance from just teachers to parents and community people. As we have already indicated, it was the PED that first mobilized William Purcell, the teacher who led the movement to change the way that the school board was elected. And Robert Cleveland, one of the three African Americans who had been elected to the board in earlier years, renewed his participation in educational issues because of the existence of the PED.[2]

Aside from the creation of such "social capital," the PED's initiative has created a system in which there is much more critical self-reflection than there was before it came into existence. In the "Theses on Feuerbach," the young Karl Marx wrote that "the educator needs edu-

---

2. He came to know about the PED through our interview with him. After initially being antagonistic to submitting to an interview with white interviewers, he became very interested in the subject matter and indicated an interest in attending PED meetings. Because he was infirm, Belden Fields would pick him up and take him to each PED meeting until his death.

cating." Through the PED, teachers learned about the perceptions that marginalized parents had of the schools. Then the PED obliged the larger system, through the mechanism of the district committee, to engage in a fact-finding and dialogical process about the way in which decisions were being made throughout the school system. It also got that system to establish norms that obliged schools to deliberately recruit members of the excluded population into their School Improvement committees in order to give voice to that often-excluded sector of the society. In this way the PED helped put into place a new mechanism whereby the system can continue to learn from its different communities.

To move from norm to practice, however, we believe that two things will be necessary—a continuation of outside pressure on the system and the system's willingness to take very concrete measures, aside from publicizing the opportunities to participate, to attract the previously excluded into the process.

The experience of the district committee's attempts to be inclusive gives us cause for concern. In our view, the system will have to adopt some very special measures to attract people. It will have to schedule meetings at times that are convenient for community people and not just for those in the school system. It will have to offer orientations and/or training to those who agree to participate. It will have to make provisions for day care and pick up transportation costs. And after it offers all of this, it may have to do something that was never discussed in either the PED or the district committee—pay people to participate.

Some might object, contending that a sense of civic duty, and a gratitude that they are even being invited in, should be enough motivation for the presently excluded. However, citizens who serve on virtually all of our representative bodies, including those who perform jury duty, are paid. The notable exception in Ed City is the school board, where members are not paid, a practice that makes it difficult for poorer people and minorities to serve. What the PED has initiated is an attempt to bring into the decision-making process people who are disproportionately poor and often holding down jobs and trying to raise children as single parents at the same time.[3] They have less disposable time and flex-

---

3. While there is unprecedented affluence in the United States, 21 percent of the work force, or 7.5 million people, were classified as "working poor" in 1997. (*A Profile of the Working Poor, 1997*, [Washington, DC: Bureau of Labor Statistics, 1997], 1.) Nearly 40 percent of the households going to the food banks serviced by Second Harvest, the largest food distributor to the poor, have full-time jobs. (*New York Times*, 19 January 2000, 21). 1990 data (the latest avail-

ibility than professionals or nonworking spouses in more affluent families. Thus, is it not reasonable to argue that when we ask the poorest segments of our population to give of their time and effort, we should offer
financial compensation? If we do not, are we not likely to see the same
class of people who presently play an active role in the PTAs and serve on
the unpaid school board serving on the school decision-making committees? Moreover, there might be a spillover effect for the school boards. If
previously excluded people were attracted onto committees in the individual schools and gained experience there, they might be more
inclined to run for school board positions. But this too would seem to
require the extension of payment, transportation fees, and child care to
members of those bodies as well. Since the time of Pericles in Classical
Athens, it has been recognized that private wealth purchases the means
to dominate decision-making bodies and that democracies, by which the
Greeks meant government of the less well-off majority, must collectively
provide such means.[4]

After spending four years of our research lives with the PED we
have come away with a conviction that the PED's efforts have already
shown results in stimulating dialogue and the growth of social capital
around public education and in making the system more reflective
about its governance. Those, in themselves, are major accomplishments.
We also come away with a guarded optimism that its efforts will ultimately result in more diverse and inclusive bodies making decisions
within the individual schools, if there is a continuation of monitoring
and pressure from outside the system itself, and if concrete steps are
taken to overcome the reluctance of historically excluded people to now
accept the invitation to come in.

---

able) for the state in which Ed City is located, reveal that in Ed City itself 12.7
percent of the population lives on income below the poverty line and that the
average annual pay is almost $5,000 below that of all U.S. metropolitan areas,
despite the high educational level of many of the citizens who are university-
related or professionals. Since these people are doing quite well economically,
there is obviously a very great income gap within Ed City. While there are a few
well-off African Americans and a greater number of poor whites, it is interesting
that the 12 percent family poverty rate in the city is roughly equal to the African
American percentage of the population.

4. See Aristotle's *Politics*, trans. Ernest Barker (New York: Oxford
University Press, 1958), 88, 171, 177, 187. For exact amounts paid for attending
the Assembly during the late period of Greek democracy (i.e., the period after
the overthrow of the Thirty Tyrants), see Aristotle's *Constitution of Athens*, trans.
H. Rackham (Cambridge: Harvard University Press, 1967), 169.

The reluctance will stem not only from the financial and time pressures noted above, but also from the fear that they might not be taken seriously, and perhaps even humiliated. Remember how two African Americans in our story felt "looked at" when they addressed or served on the school board. It will be very difficult to overcome the history of racial exclusion even in a city as liberal and as highly educated as Ed City. That higher level of education among the active white population might even make it more intimidating for the less educated in the community to accept the invitation. The African American woman in chapter 5 who was able to go to a PED meeting and tell the people there about how intimidated she felt when someone approached her to run for the school board, who said, "I'm black and everything else . . . they'll look at me and say 'another ignorant parent' " might or might not feel any more comfortable serving on authoritative bodies inside the schools themselves. The School Improvement committees, if they do attract people like her, will have to walk a rather fine line between adopting the consciously nurturing approach of the PED and a paternalism of which the superintendent was accused when he offered to assist this woman if she were elected.

Last, but certainly not least, is the issue of accountability, not that of the administrators, which we have already discussed, but of the previously excluded who might sit on the School Improvement committees. In both the PED and the district committee, a deliberative or dialogical approach was taken. That is, despite the conflict that sometimes arose in the district committee, there was a commitment to reach decisions without the adversarial method of voting. This presents us with the problem of accountability. Are we going to expect minority group members to represent some predetermined minority interests, in the form of specific policy proposals, on the School Improvement committees? Or are we going to anticipate that they will engage in a give-and-take dialogical process that would be precluded by entering the discussion with predetermined and mandated positions? Or are we going to expect them to overcome or disregard their race/class positions in favor of some unitary commitment such as "the best interest of all of the children?"

In our view, the last option will be possible only when society at large has gone much further in eliminating racial and class impediments to the fullest possible development of all of our citizens. The most pressing issue is how to resolve the apparent contradiction between the first two options, that of thinking about service on the School Improvement committees as representing pre-fixed specific positions to which members of the committee would be held by their

"constituents," or that of freely deliberating with others on the committees and coming to a consensus.

Either practically or theoretically, there is no truly clean way of
resolving this issue. But we think that the work of Anne Phillips offers a
fruitful way of negotiating the problem. Albeit directing her major attention to representation at the national level through political parties,
Phillips writes: "The only convincing basis on which representatives can
claim to speak for aspirations not yet written into their party's pro-
gramme is their relationship to organizations or movements that actively
formulate group interests and concerns."[5] The relevance to the Ed City
experience is that to avoid on the one hand being absorbed by the logic
of the system as it has functioned over time, and on the other being held
to rigid and pre-fixed positions of elements outside the system, something more than the School Improvement committees will probably be
needed. We are convinced that the "something" is a continuation of the
PED or some similar group that maintains a continuous dialogue and
activity outside of the system itself. It could relate to the School
Improvement committees by monitoring them, by bringing the issues
discussed in the various schools together to see how closely they resem-
ble each other, by raising some issues that are missing from the committees' agendas altogether, by serving as a recruiting and educative
experience for potential members of the school committees, and by serving as an advocacy group that is free of the normal constraints that often
bind those in both formal representative and bureaucratic positions. In
our view this would go a long way in dealing with John Drysek's fears of
co-optation and the drying up of such necessary organizations and
movements in the public but nonstate sphere.

But, alas, this too would entail the investment of additional time by
the citizens of Ed City, and only time itself will tell us if this way of negotiating some of the very complex issues of inclusion and democracy will
become the new version of the "Ed City Way."

---

5. Anne Phillips, *The Politics of Presence* (Oxford: Clarendon Press, 1995),
188.

References

Applebome, Peter. "GOP Efforts Put Teachers' Union on the Defensive: Reform Issues at Stake," *New York Times*, 4 September 1995, 1:7.

Aristotle. *The Politics*. Translated by Ernest Barker. New York: Oxford University Press, 1958.

———. *Constitution of Athens*. Translated by H. Rackham. Cambridge: Harvard University Press, 1958.

Barber, Benjamin. *Strong Democracy*. Berkeley: University of California Press, 1984.

Benhabib, Seyla. "Toward a Deliberative Model of Democratic Legitimacy." In *Democracy and Difference*, edited by Seyla Benhabib. Princeton: Princeton University Press, 1996.

Callan, Eamonn. *Creating Citizens: Political Education in Liberal Democracy*. Oxford: Oxford University Press, 1998.

Dahl, Robert A. "The Concept of Power," *Behavioral Science* 2, 3 (1957): 201–215.

———. *Who Governs?* New Haven: Yale University Press, 1961.

Dryzek, John. *Discursive Democracy*. Cambridge: Cambridge University Press, 1990.

———. "Political Inclusion and the Dynamics of Democratization," *American Political Science Review* 90, 1 (1996):475–487.

Hirst, Paul. *Associative Democracy*. Amherst: University of Massachusetts Press, 1994.

Horace Mann Companies. *Survey on Attitudes Toward Public Schools*, 20–22 August 1999.

Mansbridge, Jane. *Beyond Adversary Democracy*. Chicago: University of Chicago Press, 1980.

National Commission on Excellence in Education. *A Nation at Risk: The Importance for Education Reform*. Washington, DC: U.S. Department of Education, 1983.

Phillips, Anne. *The Politics of Presence*. Oxford: Clarendon Press, 1995.

A Profile of the Working Poor. Washington, DC: Bureau of Labor Statistics, 1997.

Putnam, Robert D. *Making Democracy Work: Civic Traditions in Modern Italy*. Princeton: Princeton University Press, 1993.

Rousseau, Jean-Jacques. *The Social Contract*. Translated by G. D. H.Cole. New York: E. P. Dutton, 1950.

Sartre, Jean-Paul. *Being and Nothingness*. Translated by Hazel Barnes. New York: Philosophical Library, 1956.

———. *Critique of Dialectical Reason*. Translated by Alan Sheridan-Smith. London: Verso/NLB, 1976.

Shumpeter, Joseph. *Capitalism, Socialism, and Democracy*. New York: Harper, 1942.

Taylor, Charles. "The Politics of Recognition." In *Multiculturalism*, edited by Amy Gutmann. Princeton: Princeton University Press, 1994, 25–73.

Wirt, Frederick, and Michael W. Kirst. *Schools in Conflict*. Berkeley: McCutchan, 1977.

Young, Iris Marion. *Justice and the Politics of Difference*. Princeton: Princeton University Press, 1990.

Zeigler, L. Harmon, et al. *Governing American Schools*. North Scituate, MA: Duxbury Press, 1974.

Index